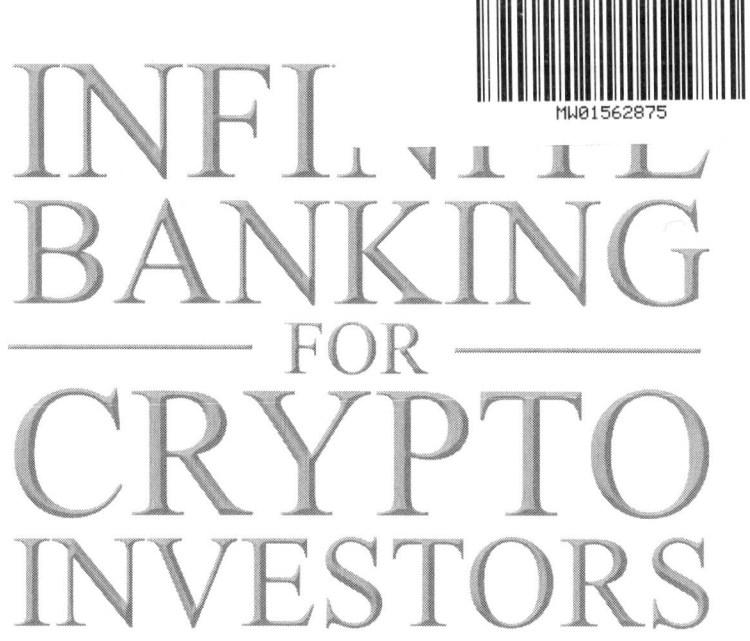

INFINITE BANKING FOR CRYPTO INVESTORS

THE OLD-MONEY STRATEGY TO BORROW, GROW AND PROTECT YOUR DIGITAL ASSETS

MAX AVERY & JAKE CLAVER

FOREWORD BY KARL VON SCHWARZ

LEGAL DISCLAIMER

The information presented in this book represents the author's views as of the date of publication. This work is intended for informational and entertainment purposes only. Due to the dynamic nature of legal, economic, and cultural conditions, the author(s) reserve(s) the right to modify and update opinions based on new developments.

While every effort has been made to verify the information contained herein, neither the author(s) nor their affiliates/partners assume any responsibility for errors, inaccuracies, or omissions. Under no circumstances should the content of this book be construed as professional, investment, tax, accounting, legal, or medical advice.

This book does not constitute a recommendation or warranty of suitability for any particular business, industry, website, security, portfolio of securities, transaction, or investment strategy. The author(s) and publisher(s) disclaim any liability for loss incurred by any person who acts or refrains from action based on the material in this publication.

Investment Considerations: The contents of this book, including any associated materials, do not constitute investment recommendations. This work does not contain all information that a prospective investor might require when evaluating an investment strategy or individual investment. Each investor must conduct their own examination of any investment strategy or individual investment, including the associated merits and risks. Prior to making investment decisions, prospective investors should consult their own counsel, accountants, and other advisors. Any discussion of past performance should not be interpreted as a guarantee of future results, and no such warranty is intended or implied.

Tax Considerations: For specific guidance on tax implications related to the subject matter of this book, consultation with a qualified tax professional is essential to ensure compliance with all relevant regulations.

Professional Advice: This communication is for informational purposes only and contains general information. The authors are not, by means of this publication, rendering accounting, business, financial, investment, legal, tax, or other professional advice or services. This book is not a substitute for such professional advice or services and should not be used as the basis for any decision or action that may affect your business or interests. Before making any decision or taking any action that may impact your business or interests, you should consult a qualified professional advisor.

Accuracy and Completeness: The author(s) and publisher(s) have made reasonable efforts to ensure the accuracy of the book's contents at the time of publication. However, they make no representations or warranties regarding the content, whether express or implied, including implied warranties of merchantability or fitness for a particular purpose. Use of this book's contents is at your own risk.

Limitation of Liability: The author(s) and publisher(s) hereby disclaim any liability to any party for any loss, damage, or cost arising from or related to the accuracy or completeness of the book's contents, including any errors or omissions, regardless of the cause. Neither the author(s) nor the publisher(s) shall be held liable or responsible to any person or entity with respect to any loss or incidental, indirect, or consequential damages caused, or alleged to have been caused, directly or indirectly, by the contents contained herein.

Legal and Tax Advice: The contents of this book are informational in nature and do not constitute legal or tax advice. The authors and publishers are not engaged in providing legal, tax, or any other professional advice. For guidance regarding the legal, tax, and financial implications of any transaction or strategy discussed in this book, you should seek advice from professional advisors, including lawyers and accountants.

By reading this book, you acknowledge that you have read and understood this disclaimer and agree to be bound by its terms.

Copyright © 2025 Trade Days Publishing
All rights reserved.

This work is protected under domestic and international copyright laws. No part of this publication may be reproduced, distributed, transmitted, displayed, sold, or used to create derivative works in any form or by any means, including photocopying, recording, or other electronic or mechanical methods, without the prior written permission of the publisher, except in the case of brief quotations embodied in critical reviews and certain other noncommercial uses permitted by copyright law. Unauthorized reproduction, distribution, or use of this work may result in severe civil and criminal penalties.

PUBLISHED BY:
Trade Days Publishing; Dallas, Texas
ISBN: 979-8-218-89862-5
PRINTED IN THE U.S.A.
Written by Max Avery & Jake Claver
Cover: Max Avery
Edited by: Max Avery & Saendy Jung

Library of Congress Subject Headings (LCSH)
Living Trusts — United States
Cryptocurrencies — Law and Legislation
Estate Planning — United States
Digital Currency
Bitcoin
Decedents' Estates
Inheritance and Succession — United States
Trusts and Trustees

BISAC Subject Headings

LAW033000 - LAW / Estates & Trusts
BUS050020 - BUSINESS & ECONOMICS / Personal Finance / Money Management
BUS115000 - BUSINESS & ECONOMICS / Cryptocurrencies & NFTs
LAW014000 - LAW / Elder Law
BUS050030 - BUSINESS & ECONOMICS / Personal Finance / Retirement Planning

About
Max Avery

After years watching crypto investors make the same painful mistake, selling positions at the worst possible times because they needed cash and had nowhere else to turn, he started asking a different question. Not "how do we get better returns" but "how do we actually keep what we've built?"

Serving as the Chief Business Development Officer and Principal of Digital Ascension Group, Max works at an intersection of technology and finance that few were prepared to occupy. What makes him different from many others in the finance space is that he actually gets why people hold these assets in the first place. The sovereignty, conviction and willingness to ride out brutal volatility because you believe in where things are headed.

He's not trying to talk anyone out of their positions. He's trying to help them keep those positions when life inevitably demands liquidity. He works off of the simple principle that the best financial strategy is the one you can actually stick with. Everything in this book flows from that idea.

About
Jake Claver

Jake Claver has spent his career asking uncomfortable questions about how wealth actually works. Not the textbook version. The real version, where families either figure out how to hold onto what they've built or watch it slip away within a generation or two.

As CEO and Principal of Digital Ascension Group, Jake oversees a firm that manages relationships with billions in digital assets. But the numbers aren't what drive him. What keeps him up at night is the gap between how much wealth crypto has created and how little infrastructure exists to protect it. Most people in traditional finance look at crypto investors and see speculation.

Jake sees people who took asymmetric bets, got them right, and now face a financial system that has no idea what to do with them. Banks don't understand them. Conventional advisors can't help them. And the strategies that worked for building wealth often fail completely when it comes to keeping it. That's exactly the problem that Jake built Digital Ascension Group to solve. Not by pulling people back into traditional finance, but by adapting the tools that have actually worked for generations to fit circumstances that didn't exist until a decade ago.

His approach is simple: meet people where they are, understand what they're actually trying to accomplish, and build systems that serve their goals.

TABLE OF CONTENTS

- Foreword i
- Introduction vii
- **The Liquidity Problem** 1
  - The True Cost of Selling at the Wrong Time 3
  - Why Bank Loans Don't Solve the Problem 5
  - Why Crypto-Native Lending Creates New Risks 8
  - Why Smart People Think This Is Stupid 9
  - Who This Strategy Is For 12
- **How Infinite Banking Works** 15
  - What Dividend-Paying Whole Life Insurance Actually Is 18
  - How Cash Value Grows Over Time 20
  - How Dividends Work 23
  - How Policy Loans Work 25
  - Why Policy Loans Differ From Traditional Debt ... 28
  - Understanding Recognition Methods 31
- **Designing a Policy That Actually Works** 35
  - The Goal Is Cash Value, Not Death Benefit 36
  - Overfunding and Paid-Up Additions 39
  - Understanding MEC and How to Avoid It 41
  - Premium Funding Strategies 44
  - Riders That Matter for This Strategy 47
  - Reading and Evaluating Policy Illustrations 49
  - Selecting the Right Insurance Carrier 52
  - The Advisor Litmus Test 55
  - Structural Flaws to Avoid 59
  - What If You Already Have a Whole Life Policy? ... 62

Coordinating With Your Crypto Holdings 67
- The Two-Bucket System 67
- Custody Choices for Securing Bucket One 69
- Timing Premium Funding With Market Cycles 73
- Using Policy Loans to Avoid Taxable Events 76
- Repayment Strategy and Timing 78
- Managing Lapse Risk 81
- The Insurance Company as Counterparty 84
- Interest Rate Sensitivity and Loan Costs 86
- Tax Considerations Specific to Crypto Investors 88
- The Execution Protocol 91
- Building Your Allocation Framework 96

Thinking in Decades 101
- What Crypto and Insurance Actually Share 106
- Planning Across Life Stages 109
- Adapting to Income Changes 112
- Estate Planning Considerations 115
- When Things Go Wrong 118
- Red Flags and Warning Signs 122
- The Infinite Banking Operating System 124

So Now What? 129

Appendix A: Glossary of Key Terms 133

Appendix B: Decision Checklist 137

Appendix C: Further Resources 141

Endnotes & Bibliography 143

INFINITE BANKING FOR CRYPTO INVESTORS

FOREWORD

This book isn't trying to sell you anything. It's here to teach you how dividend-paying whole life insurance can work as a personal financing system. It's a course specifically for people sitting on volatile digital assets. If that's your situation, you're in the right place. If not, you can close this now and no hard feelings.

The insurance industry spent two hundred years talking about death benefits while basically ignoring the living benefits. That omission always mattered, but it matters way more for crypto people because liquidity, timing, and control are what determine your outcomes. You know this already. Every entry, every exit, every tax bill that lands right when the market's down 40%. Capital access isn't some nice extra. It's the whole game.

A lot of policy holders don't understand that insurance companies already get this. They take premium dollars and put them to work every day so they can pay future claims, which means they're running a banking operation inside their general accounts. The part that gets skipped over pretty frequently is that you can do the same thing with your own money.

INFINITE BANKING FOR CRYPTO INVESTORS

Your need for financing during your life is way bigger than your need for death benefit protection. Crypto makes that painfully obvious. You need capital for entries, exits, taxes, drawdowns, patience, opportunities. Solve the financing problem and protection becomes a side effect.

Most people know you can borrow against a whole life policy. That's not news. What most people don't realize is that almost nobody funds policies at a scale where it actually matters. Small premiums mean small access, and crypto investors don't operate small. This book is about parking capital in a way that lets you move when markets give you a window.

I'll tell you something I don't love admitting. Nobody taught me this early enough, and if they had, a lot of capital decisions would've been simpler with cleaner outcomes. The reason it stayed hidden isn't that it's complicated..it's all about mindset. The financial world trains you to rent money from banks, lenders, exchanges, and margin desks. You pay them interest, they use it to fund their operations, and you never stop to ask whether you could be on the other side of that equation.

This book is for you, not for advisors. Agents should understand this stuff, but most don't. They know how to sell policies. They don't know how to build financing systems. That's a big difference, and it will cost you years if you work with the wrong person.

The goal is actually pretty simple: recapture the interest you're already paying to everyone else's banking systems. Cars, houses, education, business costs, taxes, crypto opportunities. All of those usually involve financing, which means all of those usually involve making someone else rich with your interest payments.

I should be clear about what this is and what it isn't.

It's not an investment strategy. It's a financing strategy that doesn't chase returns but instead controls the cost and availability of capital. Different problems require different solutions. Interest rates go up and down, but banking never stops. Banks often make more when rates are low because they control the flow rather than trying to predict it. You can learn to think the same way.

You'll see policy illustrations in this book and those scales change based on how the insurance company performs and what's happening in the economy, but what doesn't change is the advantage of controlling your own financing. The spread between what you earn and what you'd pay someone else to borrow matters in any environment.

This isn't a shortcut because it takes long-range thinking. I think in decades, and crypto rewards the same mindset if you can survive long enough. Intergenerational planning matters when assets move instantly across borders, especially now that the old wealth transfer rules are getting rewritten. The new rules favor people who build systems, not people who collect products.

This isn't tax-qualified, which actually makes sense when you remember that life insurance existed way before income tax did. It's a private contract between two parties solving a financial problem together, and the tax treatment grew up around it rather than the other way around. That history matters when you're trying to figure out what's actually durable versus what's just currently favorable.

There's no such thing as too much money in a system you control. Wealth has to sit somewhere, so the question is whether that somewhere gives you access on your terms or theirs. When you control your capital, you can move without asking permission, and most people never price that flexibility correctly. They see premiums as a cost without seeing the options they're building.

INFINITE BANKING FOR CRYPTO INVESTORS

I'm not talking about a bank in the normal sense. I'm talking about a personal banking system built on dividend-paying whole life insurance that, when done right, handles financing needs for your whole life. It also changes how you think about retirement. High-premium whole life does this really well when it's structured correctly.

This book is going to change how you think, and that's the point. You'll probably need to read parts of it more than once because the system is simple but probably goes against everything you were taught about money and insurance. Just know that the learning doesn't stop here. There's no point where you've figured it all out.

Other people have seen pieces of this, but few have put together a full picture for digital asset holders, and that's why Jake and Max did the work. Read it with an open mind and drop your assumptions about what insurance is supposed to be for. While you're reading it, keep one question in your head the whole way through:

> What would change in your crypto strategy if capital access was never the problem?

If that question makes you pause, then good...it should, and the answer is probably "everything."

Now go read the book.

Karl Von Schwarz
CEO, Xure Legacy
www.xurelegacy.com

INFINITE BANKING FOR CRYPTO INVESTORS

INTRODUCTION

You were there for the crash, really there, watching your portfolio drop day after day while the headlines got worse and the talking heads started using words like "correction" and "recession" and "unprecedented." You bought more anyway, hands a little unsteady, telling yourself this was exactly what long-term investors were supposed to do. And you held, through the ugly months when opening your exchange app felt like a small act of masochism, through the slow recovery that felt too fragile to trust, through the moment when you finally broke even and kept climbing. Your portfolio didn't just come back. It grew into something substantial, something that represents years of patience and a hundred small decisions not to do the stupid impulsive thing. You played this game the right way....then life happened.

Maybe it was a tax bill from last year's gains, due right when the market was down 40%. Maybe it was a down payment on a house that couldn't wait. Maybe an opportunity landed in your lap that required capital now...not next quarter.

So you sold...Not because you wanted to and not because your thesis changed. You sold because you needed cash and there was no other way to get it.

INFINITE BANKING FOR CRYPTO INVESTORS

You locked in gains you weren't ready to realize, paid taxes you could have deferred for years and gave up exposure to an asset you still believed in. And the worst part? You probably sold with bad market timing, because that's when cash crunches always seem to hit.

This is the liquidity problem nobody talks about in crypto.

Scroll through your social media feed and you'll see endless debates about custody solutions, hardware wallets, seed phrase storage, decentralization tradeoffs..and that's all important stuff. But almost nobody asks the obvious question: what happens when you need actual money and everything you own is sitting in volatile assets you refuse to sell?

Most people discover there are only three options, and none of them are ideal…

- **Option one:** sell. Convert to fiat, pay capital gains, lose your position, and hope you can buy back later at a price that doesn't haunt you. If you're taking profits on purpose, fine. If you're being forced to sell during a 50% drawdown, this is financial self-harm.

- **Option two:** go to a bank. Fill out applications, dig up income documentation, explain where your money came from to someone who thinks crypto is either fake or criminal. Wait weeks. Maybe get approved, maybe not. Banks don't understand this world and they don't want to. Even if they say yes, you've got a liability on your credit report and covenants breathing down your neck.

- **Option three:** crypto-native lending. Deposit your coins as collateral, borrow stablecoins, and hope the market doesn't move against you. When it does, and it always does eventually, you get liquidated. Your collateral sells automatically at the exact moment you least want to sell. The protocol doesn't know you've held for three years. It doesn't care about your conviction. It just executes.

None of these options let you keep your position, access cash when you need it, and maintain the control that drew you to crypto in the first place, so you're stuck choosing amongst one of the less-than-favorable outcomes you'd prefer.

This book is about a fourth option. One that's been around for over a century, but almost nobody in crypto talks about it.

The idea is simple: you build a pool of capital that you control completely and borrow against it whenever you need cash. That means no applications, no credit checks and no permission required. Maybe best of all, your crypto never moves from custody so you can capture whatever upside comes next.

The tool that makes this possible is dividend-paying whole life insurance, structured in a specific way that turns your policy into your own personal bank.

To achieve this, you fund it over time so cash value builds inside the policy. When you need liquidity, you borrow against that cash value and repay when it makes sense for you, not when some lender demands it. Meanwhile, your crypto sits untouched in secure custody.

Now, if you're thinking this sounds like a strange combination, we completely understand. Life insurance and crypto really do seem like they belong to completely different universes. Insurance is old, slow, heavily regulated, and run by institutions your grandfather would recognize. Crypto emerged from people who wanted to escape exactly those kinds of institutions. But that contrast is actually the point.

Crypto gives you asymmetric upside and real ownership of digital assets. Insurance gives you a stable, tax-advantaged pool of capital that grows steadily no matter what markets are doing. Put them together and you get something neither can deliver on its own: the ability to hold your high-conviction positions through brutal volatility without ever being forced to sell.

INFINITE BANKING FOR CRYPTO INVESTORS

What we're describing actually has a name. It's called Infinite Banking, and it was developed decades ago by Nelson Nash, a forester from Alabama who got tired of paying interest to banks every time he needed to finance something. His solution was to figure out how to become his own source of capital.

The core idea is straightforward. If you structure a whole life policy the right way, the cash value inside it becomes a private lending facility that you control.

Here's how it works. When you need money, you don't withdraw from the policy. You borrow against it. The cash value stays right where it is, continuing to earn dividends and interest. The insurance company advances your funds from their general account with your policy as collateral. You get liquidity. Your money keeps compounding. And because it's technically a loan, not a distribution, you don't trigger any taxable event. For someone holding crypto, this changes the game completely.

Instead of selling your holdings to cover a tax bill, you take a policy loan. Instead of liquidating part of your portfolio to make a down payment on a house, you borrow against cash value. Instead of watching an opportunity slip away because all your capital is locked up in volatile positions, you access funds within days and deploy them wherever they need to go. This way, your crypto stays in cold storage or institutional custody and your exposure stays intact and the upside stays yours.

That's what this book is about. We're going to show you exactly how this system works and how to implement it as someone who holds digital assets.

Here's what we'll cover:

Part One digs into the problem. We'll look at why cash flow planning matters more than portfolio optimization when you're holding volatile assets. We'll walk through why the standard solutions fail. And we'll make the case for why this approach deserves your attention even if you're skeptical about life insurance as a financial tool.

Part Two breaks down the mechanics. How does whole life insurance actually work? How does cash value grow? What are dividends and how do they get credited? How are policy loans different from every other kind of debt you've ever dealt with? This is the foundation. You need to understand these pieces before anything else makes sense.

Part Three gets into policy design. This is critical because most whole life policies won't work for what we're trying to do. They're built to maximize death benefit, not cash value. We'll show you how to structure a policy for maximum accessible capital, which riders actually matter, what to look for when choosing a carrier, and the design mistakes that turn a potentially useful tool into an expensive paperweight.

Part Four is where we coordinate all of this with your crypto holdings. Timing matters here. When should you fund premiums relative to market cycles? How do you use loans strategically to avoid taxable events? When does it make sense to repay, and when should you let loans ride? How should you think about the insurance company as a counterparty in your overall financial setup?

Part Five tackles the objections and takes the long view. Whole life insurance has a bad reputation in a lot of circles, but we'll sort out when the criticism is valid, when it misses the point entirely, and how to think about this strategy across decades of life changes.

INFINITE BANKING FOR CRYPTO INVESTORS

A few things this book won't do:

- We won't tell you whole life insurance is the best option for return on investment.

- The returns are modest compared to equities, and in the early years you'll actually be underwater as commissions get paid and the policy builds its foundation. If you're chasing yield, this isn't the place to find it.

- We won't promise quick results. Building real cash value takes years. This is a slow game that requires patience and consistent funding. If you need liquidity next month, this book can't help you.

- We're also not going to pretend there are no costs, because there definitely are. Premiums are real money leaving your pocket, loan interest adds up over time, and there's a legitimate opportunity cost to tying up capital in insurance instead of deploying it elsewhere. Anyone who tells you this is all upside is trying to sell you something.

What we WILL do is give you a complete understanding of a tool that solves a specific problem: How to access cash without selling your crypto.

If you've ever watched a position you believed in get liquidated because you needed money, this matters. If you've ever paid taxes on gains you weren't ready to realize because there was no other way to cover a bill, this matters. If you've ever felt that tension between conviction in an asset and the practical reality of needing liquidity, this book is for you.

This isn't a strategy you can implement casually. It requires capital, time, discipline, and a willingness to learn something that doesn't get discussed in normal crypto circles. It's not for everyone. But for the right person in the right circumstances, it fundamentally changes how you think about wealth entirely.

What happens is that you stop seeing crypto and traditional finance as two separate worlds and start seeing them as components of a single system that you design and control. The policy becomes your stable base while your crypto becomes your growth engine, and policy loans become the connective tissue that lets you move between them without friction, unnecessary taxes or forced decisions.

What this book is defines is exactly what real financial sovereignty looks like, and it's not just about having custody of your keys. It's about controlling your cash flow, your timing, and the choices you get to make with your own money.

INFINITE BANKING FOR CRYPTO INVESTORS

THE LIQUIDITY PROBLEM

Most crypto investors think about wealth the wrong way. They check prices, calculate gains, watch their net worth bounce around on a screen. But here's the thing: net worth doesn't pay bills. It doesn't cover tax obligations. It doesn't fund opportunities. Cash flow does.

This distinction matters more for crypto holders than for almost anyone else in the investing world, and it's worth understanding why. If you own index funds and need money, the process is pretty straightforward. You sell some shares, the price today is basically the same as yesterday, you lose a little to taxes and fees, and life goes on. It's not fun, but it doesn't feel like you just torpedoed your financial future. Crypto doesn't work that way.

The asset you're holding today might be worth 40% less next week, or it might be worth 40% more. You genuinely have no idea which way it's going to go. And because you have no idea, every liquidity decision becomes a potential disaster. Sell at the wrong time and you've locked in a loss that should have been a gain. Even if you sell at what turns out to be the right time, you've still given up exposure to something with massive upside potential.

INFINITE BANKING FOR CRYPTO INVESTORS

This is why cash flow planning matters more than portfolio optimization when you're holding volatile assets. You can have the perfect allocation, the best entry points, the strongest conviction in your positions. None of it matters if a cash crunch forces you to liquidate at the worst possible moment. The volatility creates timing risk that most financial advice ignores completely.

Think about what actually happens during a crypto drawdown. Prices fall. Your net worth shrinks. And somehow, this is exactly when life decides to throw expenses at you. Maybe the IRS wants their cut from last year's gains, calculated when your portfolio was at its peak, now due when prices have cratered. Maybe your car dies. Maybe a business opportunity shows up that needs capital now. Maybe you just need to make rent because your income is tied to an industry that moves with crypto sentiment. The universe has a dark sense of humor about these things.

Most people end up selling because they have to. They built their financial lives assuming liquidity would be there when they needed it, without ever thinking about where that liquidity would actually come from.

And this is exactly the trap. The whole game in crypto rewards those who can hold through the volatility, which means getting forced to sell at the wrong time can wipe out years of patience and conviction. But here's the thing: conviction without a cash flow plan is really just stubbornness with extra steps. Eventually something will force your hand.

The traditional financial planning world talks about emergency funds and liquidity cushions, but they're thinking about stable assets. They're imagining someone with a checking account, a savings account, maybe some bonds, who needs to cover an unexpected expense. The advice works fine for that person. Keep three to six months of expenses liquid. Done. That advice falls apart for a crypto investor.

If you're holding significant wealth in crypto, keeping three to six months of expenses in a savings account means you've got dead money earning nothing while your real assets swing wildly. And if your crypto holdings are large relative to your income, three to six months of expenses might be a tiny fraction of your net worth anyway. The standard framework just doesn't account for concentration in volatile assets.

This is why you need something different entirely. You need a liquidity source that scales with your actual wealth, gives you access without forced selling, and doesn't require you to time anything. You need cash flow infrastructure that exists independently of what the market happens to be doing.

THE TRUE COST OF SELLING AT THE WRONG TIME

It's one thing to understand conceptually that cash flow matters. It's another to see what selling actually costs you. The true cost of selling crypto to raise cash can be way worse than a lot of people realize.

When you sell, you don't just lose your position...You lose it twice. First, you lock in whatever price the market happens to be offering right now. If that price is down 40% from last month, you're crystallizing that drawdown permanently. The recovery you were counting on? You're not part of it anymore. Your conviction about where things are headed? Doesn't matter now. You sold.

Second, you give up a chunk of what you thought you were getting. The gross proceeds from your sale aren't what actually hits your bank account. Exchange fees take their cut. Slippage eats more if you're moving any real size. And then capital gains taxes take the biggest bite of all. By the time you're holding actual spendable dollars, the number is a lot smaller than the sale price made it seem.

These two losses stack on top of each other in ways that feel almost cruel. Even if your position still shows unrealized gains versus your original cost basis, the combination of fees and taxes shrinks your usable liquidity and kills your future upside. Exchanges take maker and taker fees. Spreads widen when you need to move fast. On-ramps, off-ramps, custody withdrawals, they all add fixed costs on top of percentage fees. What looks like a straightforward liquidity decision turns into a long-term wealth hit.

Let's run actual numbers:

You need $100,000 today. You decide to sell crypto to raise it.

To net $100,000 after approximately 15% in capital gains tax plus 2% in fees and slippage, you need to sell roughly $118,000 worth of crypto. That's your gross sale. You walk away with your $100,000. Problem solved, right?

Not quite.

Say the market recovers over the next eighteen months and doubles from where you sold. That $118,000 you liquidated would now be worth $236,000. You didn't lose $118,000. You lost $236,000 in future value. The $100,000 you needed actually cost you $236,000. Plus you triggered a taxable event that's going to sting again next April.

Now flip the scenario. Same need for $100,000, same market conditions, but you have a source of liquidity that doesn't require selling. You access $100,000 through some other mechanism. You pay the bill. Crypto recovers. Your position is still intact, now worth $236,000.

The cost of accessing that liquidity might have been 5% in interest over a year, maybe $5,000 to $7,000. You kept $229,000 or more in value that would have otherwise evaporated.

This is the math that changes how you think about financial structure. The gap between these two paths isn't small. It's the difference between building wealth and watching it slip through your fingers. And the gap gets wider the more volatile the asset and the longer your time horizon.

WHY BANK LOANS DON'T SOLVE THE PROBLEM

So why not just go to a bank? You need cash, you don't want to sell your crypto, and banks exist precisely to lend money to people who need it. Seems straightforward enough. That's what banks are for, right?

In theory, sure. In practice, banks create a whole different set of problems that make them unreliable when you actually need them. The core issue comes down to one word: permission.

When you borrow from a bank, you're asking for permission to access capital. You're submitting yourself to a process designed by someone else, on a timeline controlled by someone else, with terms dictated by someone else. You're hoping that a credit committee somewhere will look at your application and decide you're worthy.

That permission-based model breaks down precisely when you need it most. Here's what the standard workflow looks like when you approach a traditional lender:

You submit an application. The lender runs credit checks and pulls your financial history. Underwriters review your balance sheet, income documentation, and collateral. A credit committee evaluates the risk. They either approve or deny. If approved, you negotiate terms. Then, finally, funds show up. Every step in that process is friction & can stretch out over days or weeks.

DELAYS & DENIALS

Time-sensitive opportunities don't wait for two-week approval cycles. A market dip that creates a buying window might last 48 hours. A margin call might give you a few days. A tax deadline is a tax deadline. When the bank needs two weeks to process your application and another week to fund, the moment passes. You either sell your crypto at the worst time or miss the opportunity entirely.

BANKS CAN DISAPPEAR WHEN YOU NEED THEM MOST

Banks get nervous when markets drop. They tighten lending standards, add covenants and reduce credit limits. Exactly when you need liquidity most, they pull back. Your crypto portfolio is down 40%, and suddenly the bank that was happy to lend last year wants additional collateral or won't return your calls.

COVENANTS AND RESTRICTIONS

Even if you get approved, the problems don't stop. Lenders protect themselves with rules that limit your flexibility. Minimum balance requirements. Debt-to-income ratios you have to maintain. Asset controls that restrict what you can do with your own holdings. Reporting requirements that demand ongoing documentation. Miss a covenant and the bank can call the loan or demand immediate repayment.

Many loans restrict how you can even use the money. You might get approved for a home equity line but face limitations on using it for investment purposes. You wanted liquidity for opportunity. The bank wants to control where that liquidity goes.

Margin triggers create the worst outcomes of all. If your collateral value drops, the bank can force repayment or liquidation. This is exactly the problem you were trying to avoid by not selling your crypto in the first place. You took a loan to preserve your position, and now the loan is forcing you to sell anyway because the collateral value dropped.

The whole system is designed around the bank's interests, not yours. They're managing their risk by transferring it to you through covenants, restrictions, and triggers that activate at the worst possible moments.

Now, you might be thinking private banking is different. And you're partially right. Wealthy individuals sometimes access private banking relationships that don't work like retail lending. You build a relationship with a bank or private office. Terms get negotiated in advance. Approvals can be prearranged. That buys you speed and discretion when you need capital.

This approach has real advantages. Faster access during a crisis. Customized agreements tied to your broader financial situation. More privacy and relationship leverage.

But it has limits too. Private banking costs money. Relationship minimums are high. You're still dealing with a counterparty who has their own interests. Covenants still exist. Reporting requirements still apply. You've reduced friction, but you haven't eliminated the fundamental problem: you're still asking permission.

For someone who values the sovereignty that drew them to crypto in the first place, private banking is better than retail banking. But it's still operating within a system that requires approval, creates counterparty dependencies, and imposes ongoing obligations.

WHY CRYPTO-NATIVE LENDING CREATES NEW RISKS

Crypto-native lending looks attractive because it's fast, it's permissionless, and you can deposit your coins as collateral and borrow stablecoins against them without filling out applications, sitting through credit checks, or waiting for some committee to decide if you're worthy.

The catch is that the liquidation mechanism transfers the timing problem from you to an algorithm. When the market drops, the protocol calculates your loan-to-value ratio, and if that ratio crosses the threshold, your collateral gets sold automatically at whatever price the market happens to be offering. Which means you've essentially handed over your sell decision to a piece of code that will execute at the worst possible moment.

And it gets worse during real crashes, because market drawdowns trigger liquidations across the entire lending ecosystem at once. Everyone's collateral hits the market simultaneously, prices cascade downward, and your position gets liquidated at a price that's worse than it would have been an hour earlier since thousands of other positions are liquidating right alongside yours.

The protocol doesn't care about your thesis or the fact that you've held for three years. It doesn't factor in your conviction that the market will recover. It sees a number, compares it to a threshold, and executes.

Now, some protocols do offer better terms than others, and some have more gradual liquidation mechanisms. But the fundamental problem remains: your liquidation decision is outsourced to smart contract logic that optimizes for protocol solvency rather than your wealth preservation.

On top of all that, there's counterparty risk that people tend to underestimate. Lending protocols get hacked, smart contracts have bugs, governance decisions can change terms without warning, and regulatory action can freeze assets. The "permissionless" nature of DeFi doesn't mean risk-free, it just means the risks show up in different places.

For someone who wants to maintain long-term positions through volatility, crypto-native lending tends to create stress rather than eliminate it. You find yourself watching prices nervously, calculating how much room you have before liquidation, wondering whether to add more collateral or pay down the loan. The position you wanted to hold peacefully turns into a constant source of anxiety.

WHY SMART PEOPLE THINK THIS IS STUPID

Before we go any further, let's talk about why you should be skeptical. Whole life insurance has a terrible reputation in a lot of financial circles, and honestly, some of that reputation is deserved. Dave Ramsey tells people to avoid it. The FIRE community considers it a scam. Reddit personal finance threads are filled with horror stories about policies that underperformed for decades.

The life insurance industry is full of products designed to maximize agent commissions rather than client outcomes. Most whole life policies sold today are structured to benefit the seller, not the buyer. The illustrations look great, the fees are buried, and the cash value takes forever to build because the design prioritizes death benefit over accessible capital.

Many people who bought whole life on bad advice ended up with policies that underperformed savings accounts for the first decade. They paid premiums for years and had almost nothing to show for it. When they complained, they were told to be patient. When they tried to access their money, they discovered surrender charges that made walking away painful.

That's the bad version of whole life insurance. It exists. It's common. It's what most people encounter when they interact with the industry. What some people fail to understand is that they're really criticizing bad policy design and bad sales practices, not the underlying mechanics of the instrument itself.

A poorly designed whole life policy is a bad deal. A well-designed whole life policy structured for cash value accumulation is a different instrument entirely. The same way a poorly structured crypto investment can destroy wealth while a well-structured one can build it, policy design determines outcomes.

The critics are right that most whole life policies are bad. They're wrong that all whole life policies are bad. The difference is in the design, and most people never see a well-designed policy because agents make more money selling the bad ones.

Infinite Banking uses whole life insurance in a specific way that most insurance agents don't understand or don't want to sell.

It requires:
- Policies designed to maximize cash value, not death benefit
- Paid-up addition riders that accelerate cash accumulation
- Minimum death benefit relative to premium to push more money into accessible value
- Careful attention to avoiding Modified Endowment Contract status
- Understanding of loan provisions and their tax treatment

When structured correctly, a whole life policy becomes something the critics haven't considered: a private source of capital that grows tax-advantaged, accessible without permission, and stable regardless of market conditions.

This book will teach you how to distinguish between policies that serve your interests and policies that serve the agent's interests. You'll learn what to look for, what to avoid, and how to evaluate whether a specific policy design accomplishes what you need.

The skepticism is healthy. Keep it. But direct it toward evaluating specific policy structures rather than dismissing an entire category of financial instrument based on how it's commonly misused.

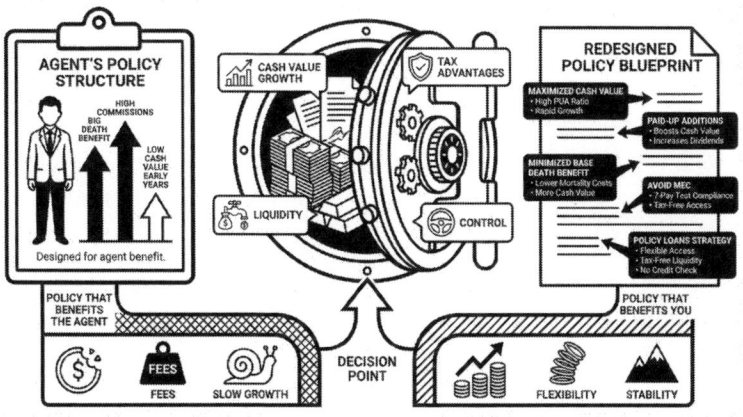

WHO THIS STRATEGY IS FOR

This strategy is not for everyone. Before you invest more time in this book, it's worth honestly assessing whether you actually fit the profile.

Infinite Banking requires:

- Stable income sufficient to pay premiums for 5+ years minimum
- Existing crypto holdings you're committed to holding long-term
- Patience to wait 3-5 years before meaningful borrowing capacity develops
- Capital beyond what you need for immediate expenses and emergencies

Infinite Banking is NOT for you if:

- You need liquidity in the next 12-24 months
- Your income is highly unstable or commission-based without reserves
- You have less than $100,000 in crypto holdings
- You're not willing to commit $6,000-$20,000+ annually in premiums
- You have no term life insurance and have dependents relying on your income

If you fall into that second category, this book will still teach you valuable concepts, but attempting to implement the strategy before you're ready will just waste money and create frustration.

Here's a simple way to think about whether you're actually ready:

- Can you commit to premium payments for at least five years without touching your core crypto holdings and without creating financial stress? If the answer is no, wait until your situation changes, because the strategy simply doesn't work if you can't fund it consistently.

- Do you have a genuine need for liquidity infrastructure? If you're not facing situations where you might need to access cash without selling crypto, the complexity probably isn't worth it. This solves a specific problem, and if you don't have that problem, simpler methods make more sense.

- Are you willing to learn something that takes time to understand? The mechanics aren't complicated once you see them, but they're unfamiliar to most people. If you want a solution you can implement in an afternoon, this isn't it.

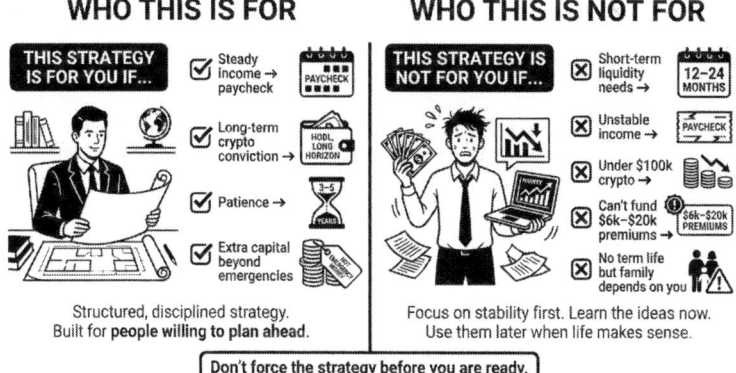

If you've made it this far and the profile fits, we're done with the convincing part. You know the problem is real, you know the standard solutions don't work, and you know you need something built for digital assets. Let's get into how this actually works.

INFINITE BANKING FOR CRYPTO INVESTORS

HOW INFINITE BANKING WORKS

Infinite banking rests on a simple insight that Nelson Nash articulated decades ago: every time you buy something, you're either paying interest to someone else or giving up interest you could have earned.

Think about it this way. When you finance a car through a bank, you pay the bank interest. When you pay cash for a car, you give up the interest that cash could have earned if you'd invested it instead. Either way, there's a cost.

Nash's realization was that you could become your own source of financing. Instead of paying interest to banks, you could build a pool of capital inside a whole life policy, borrow against it when you need money, and pay the interest back into your own system. The money stays in your system. The growth stays in your system. You're not making banks wealthy, you're building your own wealth.

The mechanics work like this:

Step One: You fund a properly designed whole life policy with regular premiums. Part of each premium goes toward the cost of insurance, which covers the death benefit, while the rest accumulates as cash value inside the policy.

INFINITE BANKING FOR CRYPTO INVESTORS

Step Two: The cash value grows through two mechanisms. First, the insurance company credits a guaranteed interest rate specified in your contract. Second, if you have a participating policy from a mutual insurance company, you receive dividends when the company performs well, and these dividends can be used to purchase additional paid-up insurance, which increases both your cash value and your death benefit.

Step Three: Once you've accumulated meaningful cash value, you can borrow against it, and this is the key mechanism that makes everything else possible. When you take a policy loan, you're not actually withdrawing your cash value. The money stays in the policy, continuing to earn interest and dividends. What happens instead is that the insurance company lends you money from their general account, using your cash value as collateral.

Step Four: You use the loan proceeds however you want. Pay taxes. Make a down payment. Buy more crypto during a dip. Fund a business opportunity. The insurance company doesn't ask why you need it and they don't have an approval process. If you have cash value, you can borrow against it.

Step Five: You repay on your schedule, which means there's no fixed monthly payment and no amortization schedule imposed by the lender. You control when and how much you repay. Interest does accrue on the outstanding balance, and unpaid loans reduce the death benefit, but nobody forces you into a payment rhythm that doesn't match your actual cash flow.

Step Six: When you repay, you're replenishing your borrowing capacity, which means the cycle can repeat throughout your life. Build, borrow, repay, rebuild.

For a crypto investor, this creates something genuinely valuable: a parallel capital base that exists independently of crypto prices. Your crypto holdings sit in custody, completely untouched, while your policy cash value grows steadily and remains available for borrowing. When you need liquidity, you tap the policy and the crypto stays exactly where it is.

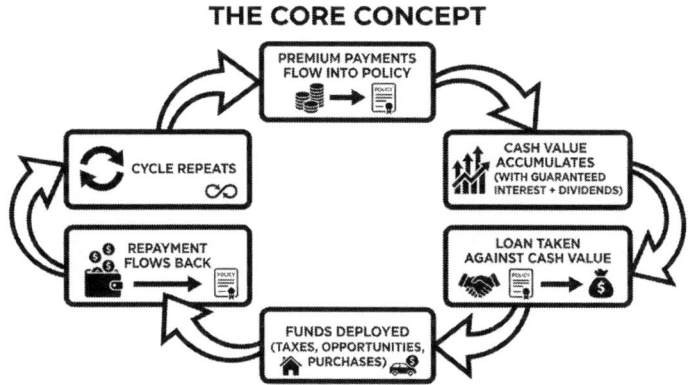

SELF-SUSTAINING LOOP: REINFORCING THE 'INFINITE' NATURE OF THE CONCEPT

The two systems work in parallel, with the crypto providing growth potential and asymmetric upside while the policy provides stability and liquidity. Together, they give you options that neither could provide on its own.

WHAT DIVIDEND-PAYING WHOLE LIFE INSURANCE ACTUALLY IS

To understand why this works, you need to understand how whole life insurance is different from other types of coverage. Most people, when they think about life insurance at all, think about term insurance. You pay premiums for a specified period, typically 10, 20, or 30 years, and if you die during that term, your beneficiaries receive the death benefit. If you don't die, which is obviously the outcome everyone hopes for, the policy expires worthless and the premiums you paid are simply gone.

Term insurance is pure risk protection. It serves an important purpose for people who need coverage during specific life stages, but it builds no value over time. It's an expense, not an asset.

Whole life insurance works differently because it combines a death benefit with a cash accumulation component. When you pay premiums, part of that payment covers the cost of insurance while the rest accumulates inside the policy as cash value. This cash value belongs to you, which means it's an actual asset on your balance sheet that you can access.

Within whole life insurance, there's an important distinction between non-participating and participating policies that you need to understand.

Non-participating policies offer guaranteed death benefits and guaranteed cash value growth at specified rates. What you see in the illustration is what you get, no more and no less. These policies are simpler but offer limited upside.

Participating policies, on the other hand, offer those same guarantees plus the potential for dividends. These policies are issued by mutual insurance companies, which are owned by the policyholders rather than outside shareholders. When the company performs well, it distributes surplus to policyholders in the form of dividends.

For the Infinite Banking strategy, participating policies are the goal for what you want because the dividends provide additional growth that can significantly accelerate cash value accumulation over time. Let's look at the components you're working with, because understanding how they fit together is what makes the whole strategy click:

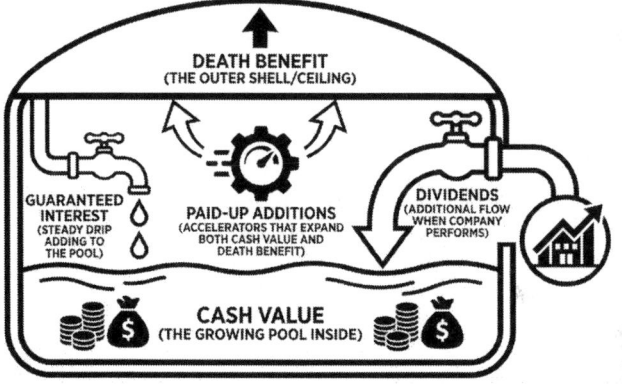

- **The Death Benefit:** The death benefit is probably the part you're already familiar with. It's simply the amount your beneficiaries receive when you die. This is the traditional insurance function that's been around forever, and while it's not the main reason we're looking at whole life for this strategy, it's still part of the package.

- **The Cash Value:** The cash value is where things get interesting for our purposes. Think of it as an internal account that builds up over time as you pay premiums, earn guaranteed interest, and receive dividend credits. This growing pool of money is what you'll eventually borrow against, so it's really the foundation of everything we're trying to accomplish here.

- **The Dividends:** Then you've got dividends, which are annual distributions the insurance company pays out from their surplus. Now, we want to be clear that these aren't guaranteed in any legal sense, but what gives us comfort is that many of the established mutual insurers have been paying them consistently for over a century. When you receive dividends, you can take them as cash, use them to offset your premium payments, or funnel them into paid-up additions.

- **Paid-Up Additions (PUAs):** Paid-up additions deserve some attention because they're the secret sauce for accelerating growth. PUAs are essentially small chunks of additional whole life insurance that you purchase using either your dividends or extra premium payments beyond the base amount. What makes them so valuable is that they immediately boost both your cash value and your death benefit, which is why they're the primary tool for turbocharging a policy designed for Infinite Banking.

What really creates the opportunity here is how all these pieces interact with each other. Your premium payments steadily build cash value month after month, dividends compound on top of that base, and PUAs accelerate the whole process even further. Over time, this combination produces a substantial pool of capital that you can tap into through policy loans whenever the need arises.

HOW CASH VALUE GROWS OVER TIME

With those fundamentals in place, let's zoom in on how your cash value actually grows. There are three sources that drive your cash value growth, and they all work together in ways that amplify each other. Once you understand how each one contributes, you'll see why the compounding gets so powerful over time.

- First, your premiums form the foundation of everything. Your regular payments are what fund the policy in the first place, and without consistent funding, nothing else really matters. The size and frequency of those premium payments basically determine how much raw material you're giving the policy to work with.

- On top of that, you've got guaranteed interest providing a floor for your returns. Your contract spells out a minimum crediting rate, usually somewhere in the 3-4% range, and this is the return you can count on no matter what's happening in the markets or how the company is performing. It's baked into the contract, which means the insurance company owes it to you regardless of circumstances.

- Then there are dividends, which is where the additional upside comes from. When the insurance company has a good year, they share that surplus with participating policyholders. The actual dividend rate bounces around from year to year based on how the company performs and broader economic conditions, but many of the established mutual insurers have averaged somewhere in the 5-6% range or higher over extended periods.

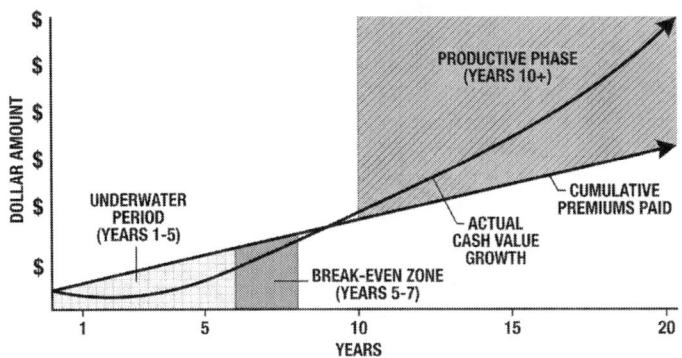

INFINITE BANKING FOR CRYPTO INVESTORS

These components compound together. Consider a simplified example:

You start with $10,000 in cash value. The guaranteed rate is 3%. The dividend rate for this year is 5%, for a total of 8%.

Year 1: $10,000 × 1.08 = $10,800 **Year 2:** $10,800 × 1.08 = $11,664 **Year 3:** $11,664 × 1.08 = $12,597

That's $2,597 in growth from an initial $10,000, assuming you add no additional premiums. Now add annual premium payments and the compounding really starts to pick up speed.

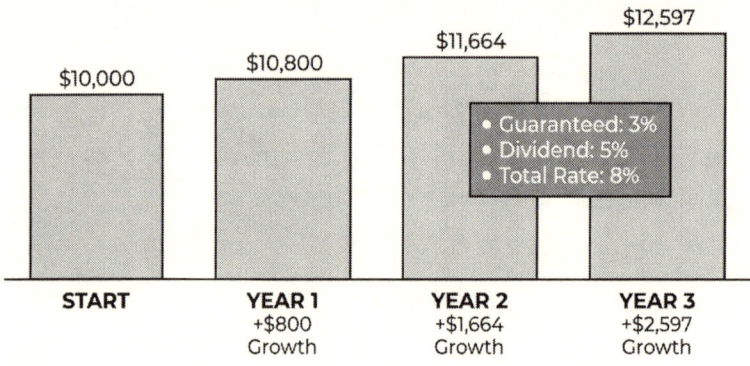

Now we should be upfront about something: the early years of a policy typically show slow growth, and you might even be underwater relative to what you've paid in. This happens because insurance companies tend to front-load certain costs, agent commissions take a bite out of early cash value, and the policy simply needs time to build momentum.

Here's what the timeline typically looks like:

Years 1-3: Your cash value will typically be less than the premiums you've paid. You might put in $50,000 over that period and only have $35,000 to $40,000 in accessible cash value. This is completely normal, and you shouldn't expect to borrow any meaningful amount during this phase.

Years 4-5: When your cash value approaches or finally exceeds what you've paid in cumulative premiums. This is when the policy starts working for you, and your borrowing capacity becomes practically useful.

Years 6-10: This is when the compounding really kicks into gear. Cash value grows faster than your premium contributions, and the gap keeps widening in your favor. At this point, your borrowing capacity reaches levels that can actually address real liquidity needs.

Years 10+: The policy enters what I'd call its productive phase. Compounding has had enough time to do its thing, and your cash value may be significantly higher than everything you've paid in. This is when the strategy actually delivers on its promise.

This timeline is exactly why the strategy demands patience. You're not building something to solve liquidity problems in the next couple of years. You're building infrastructure that's going to serve you for decades.

HOW DIVIDENDS WORK

Let's talk about dividends, because most people get confused here and it actually matters quite a bit for how this whole thing works.

So where does the money actually come from? Insurance companies generate surplus in two main ways. When fewer policyholders die than the actuaries predicted, the company pays out less in claims than expected. And then there's the investment income from all those assets sitting in their general account. When both of those result in a profit for a given year, participating policyholders get a piece of that surplus in the form of dividends.

Now here's the thing you need to understand: these dividends aren't guaranteed. A company might pay out generously one year and then cut back the next, depending on how things shake out. And if you zoom out over the past few decades, dividend rates across the industry have generally trended downward as interest rates fell. A company that was averaging 8% back in the 1990s might be closer to 5% today. Past performance really doesn't tell you what's coming next.

Having said that, what does give us some confidence is the track record. Many of these mutual insurance companies have been paying dividends consistently for over a hundred years. We're talking through world wars, the Great Depression, the 2008 financial crisis. That kind of staying power means something when you're deciding where to park capital for the long haul.

Once dividends get credited to your policy, you've got a few different options for what to do with them:

- **Take cash:** The dividend leaves your policy and enters your bank account. Simple, but removes compounding potential.

- **Reduce premiums:** The dividend offsets future premium payments. Good for cash flow management, but slows growth.

- **Accumulate at interest:** The dividend sits in a side account earning interest. Provides flexibility but doesn't maximize growth.

- **Purchase paid-up additions:** The dividend buys additional fully-paid whole life insurance that immediately adds to your cash value and death benefit.

For Infinite Banking, that last option is almost always where you want to go. The reason is that each PUA you purchase becomes its own little piece of insurance that generates its own future dividends. So you're creating this compounding effect where dividends buy more insurance, which earns more dividends, which buys more insurance. The acceleration builds on itself over time.

To really see the difference, think about two identical policies over 20 years. Policy A takes dividends as cash every year, so the cash value only grows from premiums and the guaranteed interest rate. Policy B reinvests everything as paid-up additions, meaning the cash value grows from premiums, guaranteed interest, dividends, and then the additional dividends those PUAs generate on top of that.

The gap between these two methods starts small and then just keeps widening. By year 20, Policy B could easily have 30-50% more cash value than Policy A, depending on how dividend rates play out and how the policy was designed from the start.

HOW POLICY LOANS WORK

Policy loans are what make the entire strategy practical. They're the mechanism that turns cash value into usable liquidity without selling anything or triggering taxable events.

Here's what actually happens when you take one out:

- You request a loan from the insurance company. You specify the amount you want, up to a percentage of your available cash value (typically 90% or more), and the company doesn't ask why you need it. They don't check your credit. They don't require income documentation. The contract gives you the right to borrow against your cash value, and they simply honor that contract.

- The insurance company advances you funds. Most people are surprised to learn that the money comes from the company's general account rather than from your policy's cash value directly. This matters because your cash value remains in the policy, continuing to earn guaranteed interest and potentially dividends even while you have a loan outstanding.

- Your cash value serves as collateral. The loan is secured by your policy, so if you don't repay, the insurance company eventually recovers the amount from your death benefit or cash value. Since there's essentially no risk to the company, there's no underwriting needed. They're not taking a chance on you.

- Interest accrues on the loan. Policy loan rates vary by company and contract but typically range from 5-8%. Some policies offer fixed rates specified in the contract while others use variable rates tied to market indices. If you don't pay the interest as it accrues, it compounds over time and gets added to your loan balance.

- You repay on your terms. There's no mandatory payment schedule, which gives you real flexibility. You can pay interest only, pay nothing and let interest capitalize, or pay the entire balance whenever you want. The insurance company doesn't impose a repayment cadence, so you control timing completely.

- Unpaid loans reduce the death benefit. If you borrow $100,000 and never repay, your death benefit shrinks by $100,000 plus accumulated interest. This is the tradeoff for accessing liquidity during your lifetime. For some people that tradeoff makes perfect sense, while for others preserving the full death benefit is a priority. It really depends on what you're trying to accomplish.

The tax treatment is crucial here, and it's worth pausing on this point because it's a big part of why this strategy works. Policy loans are not taxable events because you're borrowing, not withdrawing.

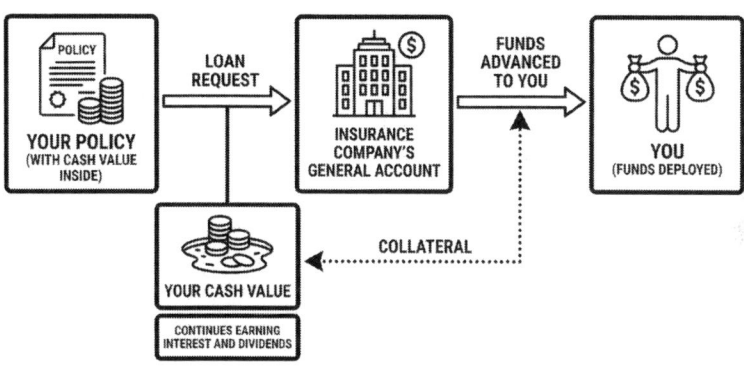

The cash value stays in the policy, so there's no distribution to tax. You receive money without triggering capital gains, income tax, or any other tax consequence. This changes the liquidity calculus entirely. To see why, compare these two tactics side by side:

Selling crypto to raise $100,000:

- Trigger capital gains tax (potentially $15,000-$24,000 depending on rate and gain)
- Lose future upside on the sold position
- Pay exchange fees
- Net much less than $100,000 in usable funds

Taking a policy loan for $100,000:

- No taxable event
- Pay interest (5-8% annually on outstanding balance)
- Crypto position unchanged, retaining all future upside
- Full $100,000 available for use

The math usually favors the loan, especially if you believe in the long-term upside of your crypto holdings. You're essentially paying a modest interest rate to preserve an asset you think will appreciate significantly over time.

WHY POLICY LOANS DIFFER FROM TRADITIONAL DEBT

Now that you understand the basic mechanics of how policy loans work, it's worth digging into why they're so different from other forms of borrowing. Because once you see how policy loans operate compared to bank loans, margin loans, or any other debt you've probably encountered, you'll understand why the strategy actually works.

- **No credit check or approval process:** Bank loans require applications, income verification, credit checks, and underwriting. Policy loans require none of this. The contract specifies your right to borrow, and the company simply honors that contract. Your credit score, income, and overall financial situation are completely irrelevant to whether you get the money.

- **No fixed repayment schedule:** Bank loans come with amortization schedules, monthly payments, and penalties for late payment. Policy loans, on the other hand, have no required payments at all. Interest accrues on the balance, but nobody forces you to pay on any particular timeline. You decide when and how much to repay based entirely on your own circumstances.

- **No covenants or restrictions:** Bank loans often include covenants that restrict your behavior, things like maintaining certain financial ratios, avoiding additional debt, or reporting changes in your financial situation. Policy loans come with none of these strings attached. You can use the money for whatever you want, and the insurance company doesn't monitor what you do with it or care where it goes.

- **No margin calls or forced liquidation:** This is a big one if you've ever dealt with margin loans or crypto lending platforms. Those arrangements can force liquidation when your collateral value drops below certain thresholds. Policy loans simply can't do that to you. Your cash value is the collateral, and because its value doesn't fluctuate with external markets, the insurance company has no mechanism to force you to repay or sell anything.

- **No impact on credit score:** Bank loans show up on your credit report and affect your credit profile. Policy loans exist as a liability within your policy but remain completely invisible to credit bureaus. Nobody looking at your credit history would have any idea you've borrowed against your policy.

- **Privacy:** Bank loans create records that various parties can access under different circumstances. Policy loans exist only between you and the insurance company, with no public records and no third-party access to the information.

WHY POLICY LOANS DIFFER FROM TRADITIONAL DEBT

FACTOR	BANK LOAN	POLICY LOAN
CREDIT CHECK	YES	NO
INCOME VERIFICATION	YES	NO
APPROVAL TIME	WEEKS	DAYS
FIXED PAYMENTS	RIGID SCHEDULE	FLEXIBLE
MARGIN CALL RISK	HIGH RISK	PROTECTED
IMPACT ON CREDIT	IMPACTS SCORE	INVISIBLE

The flexibility is really the key advantage here, especially when you think about how crypto income actually works in practice. Your cash flow might be wildly irregular. You might have a windfall after a token sale or a profitable exit, followed by months of much lower income. A rigid bank repayment schedule simply doesn't accommodate that reality, whereas a policy loan bends to fit your situation.

What this means practically is that you can let a loan sit for years if that makes sense for where you are financially. You can pay it down aggressively when you have excess cash on hand. You can pay interest only to keep the balance stable while preserving your liquidity for other uses. The decision about how to handle repayment is entirely yours to make based on what's actually happening in your life.

UNDERSTANDING RECOGNITION METHODS

There's one more technical detail about policy loans that affects long-term performance, and it's something most people never hear about until it's too late to do anything about it. It comes down to how the insurance company handles dividend crediting when you have an outstanding loan. This is called the "recognition method," and while it might sound like arcane insurance jargon, understanding it can mean the difference between a policy that maintains its momentum while you borrow and one that stalls out every time you take a loan.

> **Non-direct recognition:** With this approach, the insurance company calculates dividends as if no loan were outstanding. So if you have $100,000 in cash value and a $50,000 loan, dividends are still calculated on the full $100,000. Your policy's growth momentum stays intact regardless of how much you're borrowing at any given time. The loan exists as a separate liability on the books, but it doesn't touch your dividend crediting at all.
>
> **Direct recognition:** This works quite differently. The insurance company reduces the dividend base by the amount you've borrowed. Using the same scenario with $100,000 in cash value and a $50,000 loan, dividends now get calculated only on $50,000. What this means is that your policy earns less while the loan is outstanding, and the more you borrow, the more your growth slows down.

The difference between these two methods compounds over time in ways that really add up. Even a few percentage points of reduced annual crediting, sustained over a decade of active borrowing, creates a substantial gap in available cash value.

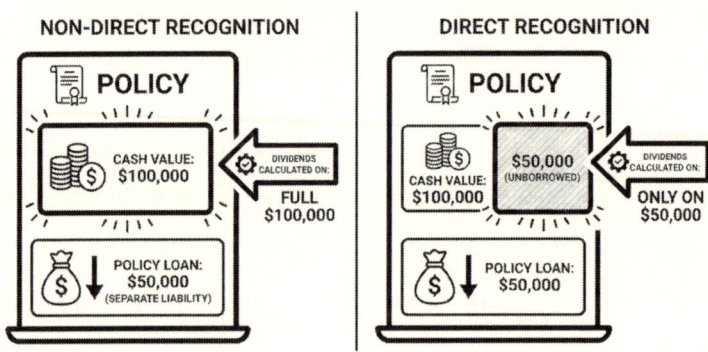

You might be wondering why insurance companies would use direct recognition in the first place. The answer is that it protects their margins. When you borrow against your policy, the company's asset mix changes because they're advancing you cash while your cash value remains on their books. Direct recognition essentially shifts some of that cost back to you as the policyholder.

To be clear, there's nothing illegal or hidden about this. It's simply a contract-level design choice that varies from carrier to carrier. The problem is that most agents don't bother to explain it, and most buyers don't know they should be asking about it.

For someone planning to use policy loans actively, as you would with Infinite Banking, non-direct recognition policies are generally the way to go. You want the freedom to borrow without penalty when markets create opportunities or when you need liquidity for whatever reason. Direct recognition adds friction to every single loan decision you'll make over the life of the policy.

Before committing to any policy, make sure you ask specifically about the recognition method and get the answer in writing. If you're comparing carriers and one offers non-direct recognition while another doesn't, that's a meaningful advantage you should factor into your decision.

INFINITE BANKING FOR CRYPTO INVESTORS

DESIGNING A POLICY THAT ACTUALLY WORKS

Now that you understand how policy loans work and why the recognition method matters, we need to talk about something that trips up almost everyone who looks into this strategy: most whole life policies on the market simply won't work for what you're trying to do. They're designed to maximize death benefit rather than cash value, and they're built to generate commissions for the agent rather than borrowing power for you. The whole structure reflects what insurance companies want to sell, which means if you walk in without knowing what to ask for, you'll almost certainly end up with a policy that doesn't serve your actual goals.

This matters more than you might think, because a poorly designed policy will just sit there for a decade accumulating nothing useful while you watch opportunities pass you by. You'll pay your premiums faithfully, check your annual statements, and keep wondering why the cash value grows so slowly. The answer is almost always the same: bad design from the start.

What really drives this home is that two policies from the exact same insurance company, funded with the exact same premium, can produce dramatically different outcomes depending on how they're structured. One might give you meaningful borrowing capacity by year five, while the other could take fifteen years to reach that same point. Same company, same money going in but with completely different results coming out.

The difference comes down to a few key factors: how premiums get allocated between death benefit and cash value, how aggressively paid-up additions are used in the design, and whether the policy was optimized for the agent's commission check or for your actual goals.

One way to think about it is that the insurance product itself is just the raw material. The design is what you actually build with that material. You can take quality lumber and construct a solid house that serves you for decades, or you can waste it on a structure that falls apart under pressure. Same materials in both cases, but completely different outcomes based on how they're assembled.

The chapters that follow will teach you what a well-designed policy actually looks like in practice. You'll come to understand the specific structural choices that accelerate cash value growth, along with the common mistakes that undermine the whole strategy. By the time you're done, you'll be able to look at any policy illustration and quickly determine whether it actually serves your interests or just the interests of whoever's selling it to you.

THE GOAL IS CASH VALUE, NOT DEATH BENEFIT

Everything we've covered so far leads to one central question: how do you design a policy that actually does what you need it to do? The fundamental design principle for Infinite Banking is simple: maximize the percentage of every premium dollar that flows into accessible cash value.

Traditional whole life policies do the opposite. They maximize death benefit per premium dollar because that's what most buyers think they want and what generates the highest commissions. More death benefit

DESIGNING A POLICY THAT ACTUALLY WORKS | 37

means more premium going toward insurance costs and less toward cash accumulation.

For your purposes, you want the minimum death benefit that allows maximum premium funding. This flips the conventional approach. Here's why it matters mathematically:

Traditional design (death benefit focused):

- $20,000 annual premium
- $1,000,000 death benefit
- High percentage of premium covers mortality costs
- **Year 5 cash value: ~$60,000-$70,000**

Cash value focused design:

- $20,000 annual premium
- $400,000 death benefit
- Lower percentage covers mortality costs
- **Year 5 cash value: ~$85,000-$95,000**

Same premium, dramatically different cash value. The difference comes down to how much of each dollar gets eaten by insurance costs versus how much actually lands in your cash value account.

THE GOAL IS CASH VALUE, NOT DEATH BENEFIT
ANNUAL PREMIUM: $20,000

TRADITIONAL DESIGN (DEATH BENEFIT FOCUSED) — CASH VALUE, MORTALITY COSTS, ADMINISTRATIVE EXPENSES

OBVIOUS DESIGN DIFFERENCE: CASH VALUE MAXIMIZATION

CASH VALUE FOCUSED DESIGN — MORTALITY COSTS, ADMINISTRATIVE EXPENSES, CASH VALUE

YEAR 5 CASH VALUE: ~$60,000-70,000

YEAR 5 CASH VALUE: ~$85,000-95,000

When you reduce the death benefit relative to premium, more of each dollar flows into cash value from day one, which means the policy builds borrowing capacity faster and you reach useful liquidity much sooner than you would with a traditional design.

Now, this doesn't mean death benefit is irrelevant to the equation. You still get permanent life insurance protection, and if you die, your beneficiaries receive the death benefit minus any outstanding loans. The coverage serves its purpose just fine. You're simply choosing not to over-buy it at the expense of the liquidity feature that drew you to this strategy in the first place.

Ultimately, the design should reflect your actual priorities. If you need $2 million in death benefit for estate planning reasons, that's a completely legitimate goal and the policy should be structured accordingly. On the other hand, if your primary goal is creating a private liquidity facility, then death benefit becomes secondary to cash value accumulation, and your policy design should reflect that reality.

One thing I'd strongly encourage is being explicit about this with any advisor you work with. If they keep pushing higher death benefits after you've clearly explained what you're trying to accomplish, that's a signal they're optimizing for their commission rather than your outcome, and you should probably look elsewhere for guidance.

OVERFUNDING AND PAID-UP ADDITIONS

We just established that the goal is maximizing cash value per premium dollar. So how do you actually do that? The most powerful tool for accelerating cash value growth is overfunding through paid-up additions, and once you understand how this works, you'll see why it's so central to the whole strategy.

- **What overfunding means:** You pay premiums beyond the base amount required to keep the policy in force, and that excess flows directly into cash value rather than covering insurance costs.

- **What paid-up additions are:** These are small chunks of fully paid-up whole life insurance that you purchase with extra premium dollars or dividends. Each PUA immediately adds to both your cash value and death benefit, but what makes them really valuable is that each one generates its own future dividends, which creates a compounding effect that builds on itself over time.

One way to think about it is that your base premium keeps the policy running and builds cash value slowly, while your PUA contributions act as turbo fuel that accelerates growth dramatically. Here's how premium typically flows in a well-designed policy:

Base premium: Covers mortality costs, administrative expenses, and builds guaranteed cash value at the contract rate.

PUA premium: Goes almost entirely into cash value (minus a small charge). This is where the real acceleration happens.

INFINITE BANKING FOR CRYPTO INVESTORS

To give you a sense of what this looks like in practice, a properly designed policy for Infinite Banking might have a base premium of $6,000 and allow PUA contributions up to $14,000, for a total annual outlay of $20,000. The ratio between these two numbers really matters, because you want maximum PUA capacity relative to base premium.

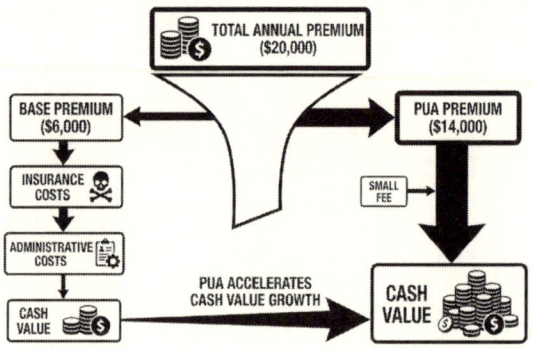

The PUA rider is what makes all of this possible. It's an add-on to the base policy that permits these additional contributions, and without it, you're limited to the base premium schedule with no way to accelerate.

WHY PUAS ACCELERATE GROWTH:

- **They bypass most insurance costs:** Almost all of a PUA dollar goes straight to cash value.

- **They earn dividends immediately:** Unlike base premium, which takes time to build dividend-earning cash value, PUAs start earning from day one.

- **They compound:** PUA dividends can purchase more PUAs, which earn more dividends, which creates exponential growth over time.

- **They increase borrowing capacity faster:** More cash value means more you can borrow against.

To put some numbers on this, a policy funded at just the base premium level might take 15 years to build $100,000 in cash value. The same policy with aggressive PUA funding might reach that point in 6-8 years.

And because we're talking about compounding, the difference only grows more pronounced over time. By year 20, the gap between minimum-funded and maximum-funded policies becomes enormous.

UNDERSTANDING MEC AND HOW TO AVOID IT

All of this talk about overfunding and maximizing PUA contributions might have you thinking you should dump as much money into the policy as possible. But there's a limit to how aggressively you can fund a whole life policy, and this is something you really need to understand before you start writing checks. If you push too much money in too fast, the IRS reclassifies the policy as a Modified Endowment Contract (MEC), which completely destroys the tax advantages that make this strategy work in the first place.

WHAT TRIGGERS MEC STATUS:

The IRS uses something called the 7-pay test, which compares your cumulative premiums against a calculated limit based on your death benefit. If you exceed that limit at any point during the first seven years, the policy becomes a MEC.

INFINITE BANKING FOR CRYPTO INVESTORS

WHAT HAPPENS IF YOUR POLICY BECOMES A MEC:

- Policy loans become taxable, so instead of tax-free access to your cash value, any loan gets treated as a taxable distribution on the gain portion.
- Early withdrawals face a 10% penalty if you're under 59½.
- The core advantage of tax-free liquidity simply disappears.

What makes this especially painful is that once a policy becomes a MEC, it can't be reversed. You're stuck with the unfavorable tax treatment forever, which is why getting this right from the beginning matters so much.

HOW TO AVOID MEC STATUS:

The key is staying below the 7-pay limit, and doing that requires careful planning from the outset.

You need to work with an advisor who genuinely understands the math here, because the 7-pay limit varies based on your age, health class, death benefit, and policy design. It's not a simple calculation you can do yourself, which means you need illustrations that show exactly how much room you have to work with.

You also need to resist the temptation to front-load too aggressively. The instinct is to dump maximum cash into the policy immediately so you can build cash value faster, but exceeding the limit even once triggers MEC status permanently. Instead, you need to spread your funding appropriately across the first seven years.

Beyond that, make sure you're monitoring your cumulative premiums annually and keeping track of where you stand relative to the limit. Your advisor should provide this information as a matter of course, but verify it yourself anyway because the stakes are too high to just trust someone else's math.

You should also be careful with single-premium policies, since paying the entire premium upfront almost always triggers MEC status. This is fine if you don't care about the tax advantages, but it completely defeats the purpose for Infinite Banking.

Finally, understand that PUA contributions count toward the 7-pay limit just like everything else. You can't bypass the test by calling excess premium "paid-up additions."

The 7-pay test is the binding constraint on how fast you can build cash value while maintaining tax advantages. You have to respect it, because the math is completely unforgiving.

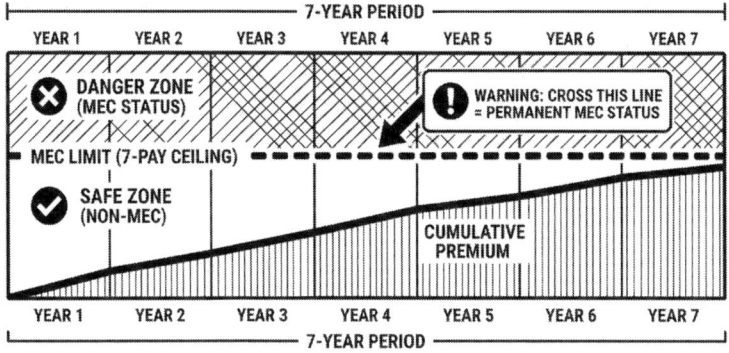

A skilled advisor will design your policy to allow maximum funding without triggering MEC status, and they'll show you exactly how much you can contribute each year along with what happens if you contribute more. If the advisor you're talking to can't explain the MEC implications clearly, that's a sign you need to find someone who actually understands what they're doing.

PREMIUM FUNDING STRATEGIES

With the MEC constraints in mind, let's look at the different ways you can actually structure your premium payments. How you fund your policy affects the economics, your loan capacity, and how the whole thing coordinates with your crypto strategy. There are several paths that you can take, and each one comes with its own set of tradeoffs worth understanding.

SINGLE PREMIUM FUNDING

This is where you pay everything upfront in one lump sum. Cash value builds immediately, and loan capacity becomes available right away.

Advantages:

- Rapid cash value accumulation
- Immediate access to borrowing capacity
- Simpler administration overall

Disadvantages:

- Large cash outflow all at once
- Almost always triggers MEC status, which eliminates the tax advantages
- Not suitable for Infinite Banking unless you genuinely don't care about tax-free loans

Single premium policies can work for certain estate planning purposes, but they're generally not what you want for this particular strategy.

LEVEL ANNUAL PREMIUM

With this strategy, you pay the same amount every year for life or for a specified period. It's predictable, easy to budget around, and matches well with stable income.

Advantages:

- Predictable cash flow requirements
- Easy to automate
- Steady cash value accumulation over time

Disadvantages:

- Slower initial growth compared to front-loaded approaches
- May not maximize cash value in the early years when you might actually want borrowing capacity

LIMITED PAY PREMIUM

Here you pay premiums for a fixed number of years (typically 10, 15, or 20), and then you stop entirely. The policy remains in force for the rest of your life with no further payments required.

Advantages:

- Accelerated funding period builds cash value faster
- No premium obligations after the pay period ends
- Works well for people who want to front-load contributions during their high-earning years

Disadvantages:

- Higher annual premiums during the pay period
- You need to maintain payments for the full period or the policy may underperform projections

FLEXIBLE FUNDING WITHIN MEC LIMITS

This method involves designing the policy to accept variable contributions up to the maximum MEC limit each year. Some years you fund it fully, while other years you contribute less based on your cash flow situation.

Advantages:

- Matches the irregular income patterns that crypto investors often experience
- Maximum flexibility in how you deploy capital
- Lets you accelerate when you have excess capital and scale back when you don't

Disadvantages:

- Requires careful tracking to avoid triggering MEC status
- More complex administration
- Underfunding too many years in a row slows cash value growth

For most crypto investors, flexible funding within MEC limits offers the best balance between structure and adaptability. Your income may be irregular depending on market conditions and when you choose to realize gains. Market timing might affect when you want to move cash into the policy versus deploy it elsewhere in your portfolio. Having the option to contribute more in good years without being locked into a rigid schedule provides valuable optionality that the other ways simply can't match.

The key is working with your advisor to understand the maximum and minimum contributions that keep your policy healthy and growing without triggering MEC status. Once you have those guardrails clearly defined, you can fund within that range based on your actual circumstances each year rather than trying to force your financial life into a predetermined schedule.

RIDERS THAT MATTER FOR THIS STRATEGY

Beyond how you structure your premium payments, you also need to think about which features to include in your policy. Riders are optional add-ons to your base policy that provide additional features or flexibility. Some are essential for Infinite Banking, others are nice to have, and many are irrelevant or even counterproductive to what you're trying to accomplish.

ESSENTIAL RIDERS:

- **Paid-Up Additions Rider:** This one is non-negotiable. The PUA rider allows you to make additional premium contributions that go directly to cash value, and without it, you simply can't overfund the policy effectively. When you're evaluating a policy, make sure you confirm the maximum PUA contribution allowed and verify that it provides meaningful room above your base premium.

RIDERS WORTH CONSIDERING:

- **Term Rider with Conversion Option:** This adds temporary coverage at a lower cost than permanent insurance, with the ability to convert it to permanent coverage later without going through medical underwriting again. It's particularly valuable if you want higher death benefit coverage now (perhaps for family protection) but can't afford the premium for all permanent insurance right away. As your situation changes over time, you can convert portions of the term coverage to permanent, which increases your cash value base.

- **Waiver of Premium Rider:** This suspends your premium obligation if you become disabled, and the policy continues as if you were paying, maintaining both cash value growth and death benefit. For someone whose income depends on their ability to work, this provides important protection because if disability strikes and you can't pay premiums, the policy doesn't lapse out from under you.

- **Overloan Protection Rider:** Some policies offer protection against lapse due to excessive outstanding loans, which means if your loan balance grows to threaten the policy's viability, this rider provides a safety net. It's useful if you plan to borrow aggressively and want protection against scenarios where you can't repay as quickly as you'd hoped.

RIDERS TO EVALUATE CAREFULLY:

- **Long-Term Care Rider:** This allows you to access the death benefit early if you need long-term care. It can be valuable for comprehensive planning, but it does add cost to the policy. Take time to evaluate whether the coverage makes sense for your specific situation and whether standalone long-term care insurance might actually be more appropriate for your needs.

RIDERS TO GENERALLY AVOID:

- **Accidental Death Rider:** This pays extra if death results from an accident. It sounds appealing on the surface, but it adds cost without improving your cash value at all. If you need more death benefit, you're better off buying more death benefit directly rather than paying for coverage that only kicks in under specific circumstances.

- **Return of Premium Rider:** This returns your premiums if you outlive a certain period. These riders are expensive and designed more for sales appeal than actual value. They reduce cash value growth to fund a benefit you don't need for this strategy.

The general principle to keep in mind is this: add riders that enhance liquidity or protect the policy's viability, and avoid riders that increase cost without improving cash value accumulation or loan flexibility.

Before adding any rider, review its impact on illustrated cash value. If adding it significantly reduces projected growth, take the time to question whether the benefit actually justifies the cost for what you're trying to accomplish.

READING AND EVALUATING POLICY ILLUSTRATIONS

A policy illustration is your window into how a policy is designed and how it's projected to perform. Learning to read illustrations critically is essential before you commit any capital, because this is where you'll spot both the opportunities and the red flags.

Every illustration shows the same basic components:

Guaranteed values: These are the minimums the insurance company commits to contractually. They assume zero dividends and the guaranteed minimum interest rate, which means the policy will perform at least this well regardless of company performance or economic conditions.

Illustrated values: These show projected performance assuming current dividend rates continue. They represent the insurance company's estimate of likely outcomes, not guarantees, so actual results could end up better or worse than what you see on paper.

Premium schedule: Shows what you're paying each year, broken down by base premium and any additional contributions like PUAs.

Cash value by year: Shows projected accessible cash value at the end of each year under both guaranteed and illustrated scenarios.

Death benefit by year: Shows the death benefit amount over time, which may increase with dividends and PUAs.

Net surrender value: What you'd receive if you surrendered the policy in a given year, after any surrender charges have been deducted.

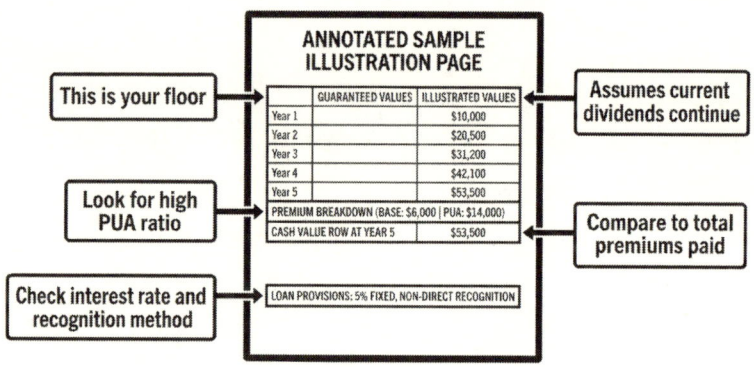

HOW TO EVALUATE AN ILLUSTRATION:

Start by comparing guaranteed to illustrated values. A large gap indicates more dependence on non-guaranteed dividends. Some gap is completely normal, but if the illustrated cash value is double the guaranteed amount, you're betting heavily on dividend performance continuing at current levels.

Next, check the early-year cash value relative to premiums. In year 5, how does cash value compare to cumulative premiums paid? A well-designed policy should approach or exceed total premiums by year 5-7, so if you're still significantly underwater at year 10, the design probably prioritizes death benefit over cash value.

You'll also want to look at the PUA allocation. What percentage of total premium goes to PUAs versus base premium? Higher PUA ratios mean faster cash value growth, which is what you're after with this strategy.

Take time to examine the loan provisions as well. What's the loan interest rate? Is it fixed or variable? What's the recognition method (direct or non-direct)? These details matter enormously once you start actually using the policy.

Beyond the standard illustration, request stress scenarios that show what happens if dividends drop by 1% or 2% from current levels. This lets you see how sensitive the projections are to dividend assumptions, which gives you a more realistic picture of potential outcomes.

Finally, ask for net-of-loan illustrations so you can see what happens if you take loans. How does borrowing affect the cash value trajectory under different recognition methods? Since borrowing is central to the whole strategy, you need to understand this before signing anything.

Red flags in illustrations:

- Projections that assume dividend rates higher than the company's recent actual rates
- No clear breakdown of where premium dollars go
- Vague or missing information about loan terms
- Resistance to showing guaranteed-only scenarios
- Pressure to make quick decisions without time to analyze

Take illustrations home with you. Study them carefully. Compare multiple options side by side. If an agent won't give you time to evaluate what you're looking at, that tells you something important about how they operate, and you should probably find a different agent.

SELECTING THE RIGHT INSURANCE CARRIER

The carrier is the counterparty holding your capital for decades. Choosing the right one matters more than almost any other decision in this strategy.

FINANCIAL STRENGTH:

Start with the balance sheet. Check ratings from A.M. Best, Moody's, and S&P, since these agencies evaluate the company's ability to pay claims and honor obligations over time.

Look for:

- A.M. Best rating of A or higher
- Stable or improving ratings over the past decade
- No recent downgrades

Ratings aren't perfect predictors of future performance, but they do provide a baseline for evaluating stability. A company with declining ratings deserves extra scrutiny before you commit any capital.

DIVIDEND TRACK RECORD:

For participating policies, dividend history matters quite a bit. When you're evaluating a carrier, dig into these questions:

- How long has the company paid dividends? The strongest mutual insurers have paid dividends consistently for over a century.
- What happened during stress periods? Did dividends drop during 2008-2009? By how much? And how quickly did they recover afterward?
- What's the recent trend? Dividend rates have generally declined across the industry as interest rates fell, so how does this particular company compare to its peers?
- Is the illustrated dividend rate consistent with recent actual rates? Some illustrations use optimistic assumptions that don't match the company's current performance.

A company that has paid dividends for 100+ years through multiple financial crises demonstrates real institutional durability. That kind of track record provides confidence they'll honor obligations throughout your policy's life.

PRODUCT DESIGN OPTIONS:

Not all carriers offer policies well-suited for Infinite Banking, which is why you need to evaluate the specifics:

- Does the company offer high PUA limits relative to base premium?
- What's the loan interest rate and recognition method?
- Are the contracts flexible about premium contributions?

- Does the company have a track record with Infinite Banking practitioners?

Some carriers are well-known in the Infinite Banking community for offering favorable policy designs. Others sell products that can theoretically work but aren't really optimized for this purpose.

SERVICE AND ADMINISTRATION:

You'll be interacting with this company for decades, so it's worth considering:

- How responsive are they to questions and requests?
- How quickly do they process loan requests?
- What's their reputation for policyholder service?
- Do they have modern online access and account management?

Speed matters quite a bit when it comes to loan requests. If a carrier takes two weeks to process loans, that undermines the flexibility that makes this strategy valuable in the first place.

CARRIER SELECTION CHECKLIST:

- Verify financial strength ratings are A or better from multiple agencies
- Review dividend history for at least 20 years, make sure to look at performance during 2008-2009
- Compare illustrated dividend rates to recent actual rates
- Confirm favorable loan provisions (competitive rate, non-direct recognition if possible)
- Ensure product design allows high PUA contributions relative to base premium
- Check reputation in Infinite Banking community
- Evaluate service quality and loan processing speed

One important thing to keep in mind: don't choose a carrier based solely on the highest illustrated values. Illustrations can be manipulated through aggressive assumptions, which is why you should focus on financial strength, dividend consistency, and favorable contract terms. Those factors matter far more for long-term outcomes than optimistic projections that may never materialize.

THE ADVISOR LITMUS TEST

Here's the reality: most insurance agents will happily sell you a policy that maximizes their commission while doing almost nothing for your cash value. They're not bad people, they're just selling what they know how to sell. Finding someone who genuinely understands Infinite Banking takes work, and finding someone who understands both Infinite Banking and crypto wealth is even harder.

This is actually one of the main reasons we built Digital Ascension Group. We kept seeing crypto investors get matched with generalist advisors who didn't understand their situation, and we got tired of watching good people end up with bad policies. Our team specializes in connecting crypto investors with professionals who actually know what they're doing in both worlds. You certainly don't have to work with us, but we've spent years building relationships with advisors who understand this intersection, and we think that network is genuinely hard to find elsewhere.

QUESTIONS THAT ACTUALLY TELL YOU SOMETHING

When you're interviewing advisors, there are a few questions that will quickly separate the specialists from the generalists.

Start by asking what percentage of their clients use policies for Infinite Banking versus traditional death benefit planning. If they stumble on this question, or if the answer is something like "a handful" or "we've done a few," that tells you they don't specialize in this strategy. You want someone who works with Infinite Banking clients regularly, because you shouldn't be paying for someone's learning curve.

You'll also want to understand how they get paid. Commission-only advisors have built-in incentives to sell products rather than optimize your structure, which doesn't automatically disqualify them, but it's information you need when evaluating their recommendations. Fee-based advisors who also receive commissions can offset some of that bias, while fee-only advisors who rebate commissions tend to have the most aligned incentives. That said, fee-only advisors who work with insurance are genuinely rare.

Another revealing question is whether they can show you an illustration that prioritizes cash value over death benefit. A competent Infinite Banking advisor knows exactly what this means and can produce it immediately. If they hesitate, push back, or seem confused by the request, that's your signal to keep looking.

Given your background, you should definitely ask if they've worked with clients who fund policies using crypto proceeds. If the answer is no, they may not understand source-of-funds documentation requirements or how irregular crypto income patterns work. Crypto wealth creates specific underwriting considerations that generalist advisors often miss.

Finally, ask what carriers they work with and why. An advisor locked into a single carrier can't really optimize for your situation, so you want someone who can access multiple carriers and explain the tradeoffs between them for your specific circumstances.

SIGNS YOU SHOULD WALK AWAY

There are certain behaviors that should make you uncomfortable pretty quickly.

- If someone is pressuring you to decide fast, that's a problem. Good advisors give you time to think because they know you're making a decades-long commitment. Similarly, if they won't show you multiple carrier illustrations side by side, that suggests they're more interested in selling you their preferred product than finding your best option.

- Watch out for advisors who keep steering the conversation toward death benefit amount rather than cash value trajectory. That tells you they're thinking about this as traditional insurance, not as a liquidity tool. The same goes for anyone who glosses over MEC limits or the 7-pay test, since those concepts are absolutely central to this strategy.

- Be especially skeptical of anyone making guarantees about future dividend rates or performance. Dividends aren't guaranteed, full stop, and any advisor who suggests otherwise is either uninformed or misleading you. You should also be wary if they dismiss your questions about loan provisions or recognition methods, because those details matter enormously once you start actually using the policy.

- And if someone keeps emphasizing fancy riders and bells and whistles rather than core policy structure, they're probably more focused on what sounds impressive than on what actually works.

WHERE TO START YOUR SEARCH

Fee-only financial planners who also hold insurance licenses sometimes work with this strategy, although they're quite rare. Referrals from other crypto investors who have successfully implemented the strategy can be valuable too. When you get referrals, ask about their experience, how the policy has performed over time, and whether their advisor explained everything clearly.

This is where Digital Ascension Group can genuinely help. We've already done the work of identifying advisors who understand both Infinite Banking and the specific needs of crypto investors. Our network includes professionals who won't be thrown off by irregular income patterns, who understand source-of-funds documentation, and who know how to design policies for people whose wealth looks different from traditional clients. You're welcome to do this search on your own, but if you want a shortcut to vetted professionals, that's what we're here for.

WHAT GOOD LOOKS LIKE

When you find the right advisor, they'll ask detailed questions about your goals, timeline, and financial situation before showing you anything. They'll explain how whole life insurance works at a mechanical level, walking you through multiple illustration scenarios including stress tests. They'll be clear about MEC implications for different funding approaches, and they'll explain loan provisions, including interest rates and recognition methods, without you having to pull the information out of them.

A good advisor will compare multiple carriers and explain why they'd recommend one over another for your specific situation. They'll give you time to think without pressure, and they'll remain available for questions after the policy is issued.

Take your time when selecting someone to work with. The care you invest in this process determines whether your policy actually works for you or becomes an expensive mistake you're stuck with for decades.

STRUCTURAL FLAWS TO AVOID

Knowing what to look for gets you most of the way there. But even people who understand all of that can still end up with policies that don't work the way they intended, usually because they walked into a trap without realizing it.

MISTAKE 1:
MAXIMIZING DEATH BENEFIT INSTEAD OF CASH VALUE

This is the most common mistake by far. Standard policy designs prioritize death benefit because that's what sells and what generates the highest commissions. For Infinite Banking, you want the opposite. Look for a minimum death benefit that allows maximum premium funding.

If your illustration shows a death benefit that's 50x your annual premium, the policy is probably optimized for death benefit rather than cash value. A more appropriate ratio for Infinite Banking might be somewhere in the range of 20-25x annual premium.

MISTAKE 2:
INSUFFICIENT PUA CAPACITY

The PUA rider is what allows aggressive funding, so if the maximum PUA contribution is small relative to base premium, you simply can't accelerate cash value effectively.

Look for policies where PUA capacity is at least 1.5-2x the base premium, and ideally higher than that. If the base premium is $10,000, you want to be able to contribute at least $15,000-$20,000 in PUAs on top of that.

MISTAKE 3:
USING OVERLY OPTIMISTIC DIVIDEND ASSUMPTIONS

Some illustrations use dividend rates higher than the company's recent actual performance, which makes projections look better on paper but sets you up for unrealistic expectations down the road.

Make sure you ask what dividend rate the illustration assumes and then compare it to the company's actual credited rate over the past five years. If the illustration assumes significantly higher rates, request a more conservative projection so you can see what you're actually likely to get.

MISTAKE 4:
IGNORING THE RECOGNITION METHOD

If you plan to borrow actively, the recognition method really matters. Direct recognition policies reduce dividends when you have loans outstanding, while non-direct recognition policies keep crediting at the full rate regardless of your loan balance.

Not all carriers offer non-direct recognition, but if you're choosing between similar policies and one offers non-direct recognition, that's a meaningful advantage you shouldn't overlook.

MISTAKE 5:
TRIGGERING MEC STATUS ACCIDENTALLY

Exceeding the 7-pay limit eliminates the tax advantages that make policy loans attractive in the first place. This typically happens when people fund too aggressively in the early years without fully understanding the limits.

Make sure you have clear documentation of the maximum annual contribution that avoids MEC status, and track your cumulative contributions against that limit carefully. This is not something you want to guess about.

MISTAKE 6:
BUYING UNNECESSARY RIDERS

Riders add cost, and each dollar spent on rider premiums is a dollar that's not going to cash value. Only add riders that directly support your goals: the PUA rider is essential, waiver of premium is often valuable, and possibly a term rider with conversion option depending on your situation.

Avoid riders that sound appealing but don't actually improve your liquidity position, including accidental death, return of premium, and most variations of living benefit riders.

MISTAKE 7:
CHOOSING A CARRIER FOR THE WRONG REASONS

Don't pick a carrier just because their illustration shows the highest values. Illustrations can be manipulated through aggressive assumptions, so what looks best on paper may not reflect what you'll actually experience.

Instead, pick a carrier based on financial strength, dividend track record through multiple economic cycles, favorable loan provisions, and policy design flexibility. These factors predict long-term outcomes far better than optimistic projections ever will.

MISTAKE 8:
WORKING WITH AN ADVISOR WHO DOESN'T UNDERSTAND THE STRATEGY

A general insurance agent will sell you a general insurance policy, and that's simply not what you need in this case.

Find someone who specializes in Infinite Banking, genuinely understands the design principles, and can demonstrate real experience with clients pursuing similar goals. The wrong advisor can set you back years with a poorly designed policy, and by the time you realize the mistake, you've already sunk significant capital into something that doesn't work the way you needed it to.

WHAT IF YOU ALREADY HAVE A WHOLE LIFE POLICY?

Many people already own whole life policies purchased years ago for traditional reasons. So a reasonable question is whether you can use an existing policy for Infinite Banking, and the answer is "maybe."

Here's how to evaluate what you have:

STEP 1: REQUEST AN IN-FORCE ILLUSTRATION

Contact your insurance company and request a current in-force illustration. This document shows your policy's current values, projected future growth, and loan provisions. Once you have it in hand, compare what you see now to what was originally projected when you bought the policy.

STEP 2: EVALUATE THE KEY FACTORS

Start by asking whether it's a participating policy from a mutual company. Non-participating policies or policies from stock companies have limited growth potential, because dividends are what accelerate cash value in a participating policy.

You'll also want to find out the loan interest rate and recognition method. Direct recognition policies reduce dividends when you borrow, which makes them less suitable for active borrowing. Check your contract or call the company directly to get this information.

Take a close look at your current cash value relative to premiums paid. If you've paid premiums for ten years and your cash value is still significantly below total premiums, the policy may have been poorly designed or sold primarily for death benefit rather than cash accumulation.

Another important question is whether you can add paid-up additions. Some policies allow additional PUA contributions while others don't, and this flexibility matters quite a bit for accelerating cash value going forward.

Finally, check what the surrender charges look like. If you're past the surrender charge period (typically 10-15 years), you have more flexibility in your options, including potentially exchanging to a better-designed policy.

STEP 3: DECIDE YOUR PATH FORWARD

If your existing policy scores well on these factors, you may be able to use it for Infinite Banking purposes. Consider adding PUA contributions if the policy allows them, since that's the fastest way to accelerate cash value growth from where you are now.

If your existing policy scores poorly, you have several options to consider:

- **Option A:** Keep it for death benefit and start a new policy designed for cash value. Your existing policy continues to provide life insurance protection, while a new policy, properly designed, provides the liquidity infrastructure you're looking for. They serve different purposes, and there's nothing wrong with having both.

- **Option B:** Execute a 1035 exchange. A 1035 exchange allows you to transfer cash value from one life insurance policy to another without triggering taxes, which means you could move to a better-designed policy. This strategy is complex and requires professional guidance to execute correctly, but it can be the right move in certain situations.

- **Option C:** Surrender and start fresh. Surrendering triggers a taxable event on any gains inside the policy, which sounds painful. But if the policy is poorly designed with minimal cash value relative to premiums, the tax hit may actually be small and worth taking so you can start over with better structure.

The takeaway here is that you shouldn't assume your existing policy works for this strategy, but also don't assume that it doesn't. Get the actual numbers, evaluate them against the criteria in this chapter, and then make an informed decision based on what you find.

INFINITE BANKING FOR CRYPTO INVESTORS

COORDINATING WITH YOUR CRYPTO HOLDINGS

You now understand how whole life insurance works and how to design a policy for cash value accumulation. So the next question becomes practical: how do you actually coordinate all of this with your crypto holdings?

THE TWO-BUCKET SYSTEM

The way we think about it is as two separate buckets operating in parallel within your overall financial architecture.

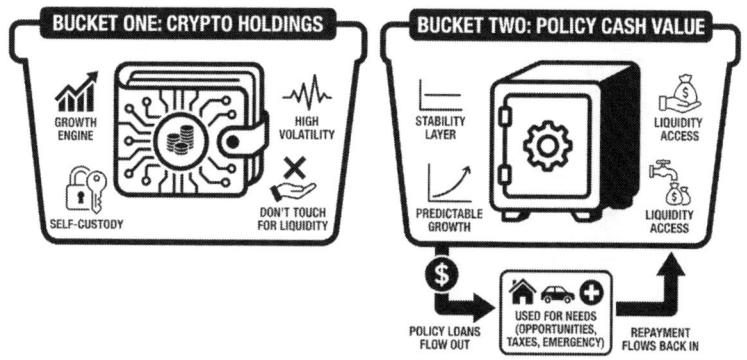

BUCKET ONE: CRYPTO HOLDINGS

This is your growth engine. We're talking about high volatility with high potential upside, along with true ownership through self-custody. These assets sit in cold storage or institutional custody, and the important thing is that they don't move unless you make a deliberate decision to rebalance, take profits, or exit a position entirely.

BUCKET TWO: POLICY CASH VALUE

This is your stability layer. You've got low volatility here, predictable growth that you can count on, and the ability to access funds through policy loans whenever you need them. This capital builds steadily regardless of what crypto markets happen to be doing, which means it provides liquidity without ever requiring you to touch Bucket One.

These two buckets serve different purposes and operate under completely different rules, and that's actually the whole point. Your crypto gives you asymmetric upside and exposure to technological change. Your policy gives you stable capital and liquidity infrastructure. When you put them together, they create a kind of optionality that you simply couldn't achieve with either one on its own.

So when you need cash, you draw from Bucket Two through a policy loan, which means Bucket One stays completely intact. Then when you repay the loan later, Bucket Two replenishes and you're ready for the next time. This cycle can repeat throughout your entire life.

What we really want you to understand is that these buckets aren't competing with each other for your attention or your capital. They're actually working together toward the same goal. The policy isn't trying to match crypto returns or replace that growth potential. Instead, it's the tool that lets you actually capture those returns by staying invested through the brutal volatility instead of being forced to sell at exactly the wrong moment.

Think about it this way: your crypto thesis might be absolutely right. The project you believe in might 10x or more over the next few years. But here's what keeps us up at night when we think about how most people have their finances structured: you'll never see that outcome if a tax bill, an emergency or some unexpected expense forces you to liquidate at the bottom of a drawdown. The policy is what lets you hold long enough for your thesis to actually play out the way you believe it will.

CUSTODY CHOICES FOR SECURING BUCKET ONE

In the previous section, we defined your crypto holdings as Bucket One, the growth engine that sits untouched while you tap your policy for liquidity. But defining the bucket isn't enough, because you still have to decide how you're actually going to hold it.

A lot of people live by the concept of "not your keys, not your coins," and for good reason. Self-custody means no counterparty risk, which means nobody can freeze your account, nobody can mismanage your funds, and nobody can collapse and take your assets down with them. You control everything.

But here's the thing that becomes increasingly real as your holdings grow: that total control introduces a different kind of risk, because you become the single point of failure.

Somewhere between 15% and 20% of all Bitcoin is considered permanently lost. Most of that comes down to lost keys or forgotten seed phrases. A house fire, a hardware wallet that gets thrown away by accident, a stroke that wipes out the memory of where you stored your backup.

INFINITE BANKING FOR CRYPTO INVESTORS

One mistake and decades of wealth vanish forever. Your heirs might inherit nothing because they can't find or access what you left them. This creates a spectrum you need to think about.

- Self-custody gives you maximum sovereignty and zero counterparty exposure. Hardware wallet options exist such as D'Cent and Ellipal that support a variety of assets and are easy to use. But it also means maximum responsibility, so if something happens to you or your backup systems, nobody can help. The blockchain doesn't have a customer service number.

- Institutional custody is a next-level solution, especially when you remember what happened with FTX, Celsius, and Voyager. Millions of people thought their assets were safely held by professionals, and they were wrong. Those customers learned the hard way that an exchange account isn't a vault. It's really just an unsecured loan to a tech company, and when that company fails, you're just another creditor waiting in line for whatever's left.

What most people don't realize is that true institutional custody is a completely different animal from keeping coins on an exchange. The problem wasn't the concept of professional custody. The problem was that those platforms never actually provided it. Even now, some companies will advertise a custody solution that doesn't fit the criteria that we consider sufficient.

What we consider true institutional custody meets five specific standards, and these are the criteria that separate real custodians from the exchange platforms that blew up and the companies that claim institutional custody without actually having the infrastructure to back it up:

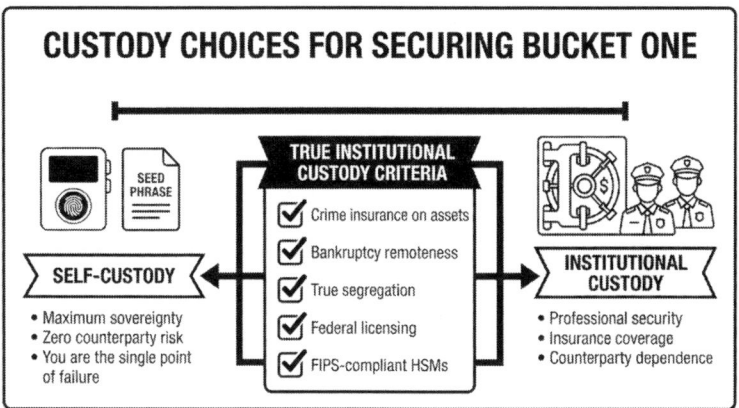

- **Crime insurance on the assets themselves:** Not insurance on their servers or their technology stack. Insurance that pays you if your crypto gets stolen through hacking, fraud, or employee misconduct. A lot of providers advertise "insurance" without specifying what's actually covered, so if the policy protects their infrastructure but not your holdings, it won't help you when things go wrong.

- **Bankruptcy remoteness:** Your assets need to be legally separated from the custodian's balance sheet. In an omnibus account structure where everyone's holdings get pooled together, you become an unsecured creditor if the company fails. FTX customers watched their assets appreciate during the bankruptcy proceedings while they waited in line with all the other creditors, getting back pennies on the dollar.

- **True segregation:** Your own wallet, your own account, separate from everyone else's holdings. Not an internal ledger entry showing your "share" of a pooled wallet. Actual on-chain separation you can verify yourself.

- **Federal licensing:** A bank charter from the Office of the Comptroller of the Currency represents the highest level of regulatory oversight in the United States. State licenses and money transmitter registrations exist too, but they're not the same thing. Prime Trust had a Nevada charter and still managed to "lose access" to customer wallets before using client funds to cover the shortfall. The regulatory framework matters.

- **FIPS-compliant hardware security modules:** Federal Information Processing Standards require qualified custodians to use HSM technology in military-grade facilities with physical security, not just software-based solutions. These are actual vaults with armed guards and encrypted sharded keys spread across multiple locations. It's the difference between a bank vault and a password manager.

Most providers in the crypto space fail at least one of these criteria. Some fail several. The ones using MPC-only solutions without HSM infrastructure can't technically qualify as custodians under US regulations, regardless of what their marketing says.

IF YOU'RE CONSIDERING THE INSTITUTIONAL ROUTE...

For investors with significant portfolios, Digital Ascension Group and its SEC-registered advisory arm Digital Wealth Partners offer custody through Anchorage Digital, one of the few federally chartered cryptocurrency banks in the United States. The arrangement meets all five criteria: crime insurance on assets, bankruptcy remoteness, segregated wallets, OCC federal charter, and FIPS-validated HSM technology.

What makes their structure particularly relevant for readers of this book is the requirement that assets be held in an LLC, trust, or IRA structure. This aligns with the broader philosophy of treating your wealth as something you architect intentionally rather than accumulate haphazardly. The same entity structures that provide liability protection and simplify estate transfer also create clean separation between your personal finances and your investment holdings.

If you're not comfortable being the sole guardian of your private keys, or if your holdings have reached a scale where the self-custody risks genuinely concern you, this is the professional alternative worth evaluating.

For everyone else, the self-custody path remains perfectly viable. Just make sure your backup systems are robust, that your estate plan accounts for key access, and that you've genuinely thought through what happens if you're not around to manage things yourself.

Regardless of which path you choose, the goal remains the same: your crypto stays secure and untouched while your policy provides the liquidity you need. How you secure Bucket One is a separate decision from how you use Bucket Two, but what matters is that both pieces of the puzzle actually work the way you need them to.

TIMING PREMIUM FUNDING WITH MARKET CYCLES

Now that we've covered how to secure your crypto holdings, let's talk about the other side of the equation: your policy. Specifically, when you fund your policy relative to crypto market conditions affects both your opportunity cost and your psychological relationship with the strategy. This timing piece matters more than most people realize.

FUNDING DURING CRYPTO DOWNTURNS:

When crypto prices are depressed, funding your policy feels less painful. The money you're putting into premiums isn't competing against a raging bull market, and since your crypto holdings are down anyway, deploying cash elsewhere doesn't feel like you're missing out on anything.

There's also a tactical advantage worth considering here. If you're funding premiums with fiat that would otherwise just sit idle in a bank account, you're actually putting that capital to work building future liquidity. When the market eventually recovers, you'll find yourself with both appreciated crypto holdings and increased policy cash value, which means you've built on both fronts simultaneously.

FUNDING DURING CRYPTO BULL MARKETS:

When prices are soaring, every dollar not in crypto feels like a missed opportunity. Premium payments feel expensive because you're measuring them against all the potential gains you could be capturing.

This is where discipline really matters. The policy isn't trying to compete with bull market returns, and you shouldn't evaluate it that way. What it's actually doing is building infrastructure for the inevitable corrections that will come. The premium you pay during a bull market is what funds the borrowing capacity you'll desperately want during the next bear market.

Some people find it easier to fund premiums using profits taken during bull markets. The strategy works like this: you sell a portion of your gains, pay taxes on those gains, and then route the after-tax proceeds into the policy. At that point, the gains are already realized and the capital has already transitioned to fiat. Directing it to the policy rather than spending it or letting it sit in a savings account puts it to productive use building your liquidity infrastructure.

COORDINATING WITH YOUR CRYPTO HOLDINGS

MATCHING FUNDING TO YOUR CASH FLOW:

The most sustainable approach is establishing a premium schedule you can maintain regardless of what the market happens to be doing. If you're committing $20,000 annually to a policy, that number shouldn't change based on the price of your crypto.

Consistency matters for several important reasons:

- The policy compounds most effectively with steady funding over time
- Trying to time premium payments creates unnecessary decision fatigue
- Stopping and starting premiums can negatively affect policy performance
- MEC limits are calculated over seven years, which requires planned contributions

Set a funding level you can genuinely sustain through any market environment. If that means starting with lower premiums and increasing them later as your situation improves, that's perfectly fine. Consistency beats optimization every time.

USING PUAS FOR FLEXIBILITY:

Your base premium should remain stable year after year, but your PUA contributions can flex with your circumstances.

In years when you have excess capital from crypto profits or other income sources, you can maximize PUA contributions up to the MEC limit and really accelerate your cash value growth. In years when cash is tight or opportunities elsewhere look compelling, you can contribute less to PUAs while still maintaining the base premium that keeps the policy healthy.

This gives you a disciplined foundation to build on, with tactical flexibility layered on top to adapt to whatever your financial life actually looks like in any given year.

INFINITE BANKING FOR CRYPTO INVESTORS

USING POLICY LOANS TO AVOID TAXABLE EVENTS

The primary tactical advantage of policy loans for crypto investors is avoiding taxable sales. Understanding when and how to deploy this advantage requires thinking through specific scenarios, so let us walk you through a few that come up regularly.

SCENARIO: TAX BILL DUE, CRYPTO IS DOWN

You owe $80,000 in taxes from last year's gains. Those gains were calculated when your portfolio was at its peak, but now the market has dropped 40%.

If you sell to pay the tax bill, you're looking at:

- Realizing whatever gains or losses exist at current prices
- Potentially creating additional tax liability if you're selling appreciated assets
- Losing exposure to any recovery
- Locking in the drawdown as a permanent loss of position

Taking a policy loan instead changes the picture completely:

- Creates no taxable event
- Preserves your entire crypto position
- Costs you interest on the loan (5-8% annually)
- Maintains full exposure to recovery

If your holdings recover to their previous highs and beyond within a few years, the policy loan path dramatically outperforms selling. You paid maybe $5,000-$10,000 in interest over that period, but you kept a position that may have doubled or more from the point where you would have been forced to sell.

SCENARIO: OPPORTUNITY REQUIRES QUICK CAPITAL

A private investment opportunity lands in your lap and requires $100,000 within two weeks. You have the capital in crypto, but selling would trigger significant gains taxes and you believe the crypto will continue appreciating.

With a policy loan:

- Funds are available within days
- No tax event gets triggered
- Your crypto position stays completely unchanged
- Interest accrues but can be repaid from investment returns

The policy loan essentially acts as bridge financing in this situation. You capture the opportunity without sacrificing your core positions, and you can sort out the repayment later once the investment starts generating returns.

SCENARIO: DOWN PAYMENT ON A PROPERTY

You're buying a house and need $150,000 for the down payment. Your net worth is substantial but heavily concentrated in crypto.

If you sell crypto to raise the funds:

- Triggers capital gains on $150,000+ of sales (likely more to cover the taxes on those sales)
- Reduces your crypto position permanently
- Creates a large taxable event in a single year

Taking a policy loan instead:

- Provides $150,000 without selling anything

- Interest accrues, but you're building equity in the property at the same time
- Crypto continues to appreciate (or depreciate) without your intervention
- You can repay the loan over time as cash flow allows

When selling might make more sense:

Policy loans aren't always the right answer, and it's worth being honest about that.

Consider selling instead when:

- You've decided to reduce your crypto allocation anyway for portfolio reasons
- The tax bill from selling would be minimal because you have low cost basis holdings or losses to offset
- Interest rates on policy loans exceed your expected return on the assets
- You don't have sufficient cash value to borrow what you need
- You need to deleverage for risk management reasons

The decision framework is actually pretty straightforward once you lay it out: if preserving your crypto position has value because you expect it to appreciate, and the cost of the policy loan is less than the expected appreciation plus the taxes you're avoiding, then the loan is the better path. When those conditions don't hold, selling might actually make more sense for your situation.

REPAYMENT STRATEGY AND TIMING

Taking policy loans is only half the equation. How and when you repay those loans affects both your policy's health and your overall financial position. There's no single right answer here, but there are principles that can guide your decisions.

THE FLEXIBILITY IS THE POINT:

Unlike bank loans with fixed payment schedules, policy loans let you repay on your own terms. You can pay interest only to maintain the principal balance, pay nothing and let interest capitalize, make irregular payments whenever cash becomes available, or pay off the entire balance at once if that makes sense for your situation.

This flexibility is what lets you match repayments to your actual cash flow rather than trying to conform to some lender's arbitrary requirements.

REPAYING DURING CRYPTO RECOVERIES:

The logical time to repay policy loans is when your crypto holdings have recovered or appreciated significantly. You might take some profits during a bull market, use those proceeds to pay down your policy loans, and then rebuild your borrowing capacity for the next cycle.

What this creates is a natural rhythm: you borrow during downturns or when opportunities arise, then repay during periods of strength. The policy becomes a tool for managing crypto's volatility rather than being whipsawed by it.

INTEREST CONSIDERATIONS:

Loan interest compounds if you leave it unpaid, which is something you need to factor into your planning. A $100,000 loan at 6% grows to $106,000 after one year if you make no payments at all. After five years with no payments, that balance has grown to roughly $134,000.

Now, this compounding isn't necessarily a bad thing. If your crypto position grows faster than 6% annually, letting the loan ride while staying invested actually produces a positive spread in your favor. But the math can definitely work against you if markets stagnate or decline for extended periods.

One approach worth considering is paying at least the interest annually to prevent the balance from growing. This maintains your borrowing capacity and keeps the policy healthy without requiring large principal payments that might strain your cash flow.

SETTING REPAYMENT TRIGGERS:

Rather than deciding on an ad hoc basis when to repay, we'd suggest establishing rules in advance that take the guesswork out of it:

"When my crypto portfolio exceeds $X, I'll repay 25% of outstanding policy loans from profits."

"Each quarter, I'll pay at least the accrued interest on any policy loans."

"When my portfolio reaches $Y, I'll pay off all policy loans to reset my borrowing capacity."

The beauty of predefined triggers is that they remove emotion from the decision entirely. You're not trying to time the market or second-guess yourself. You're simply executing a plan based on observable conditions that you defined when you were thinking clearly.

WHAT IF YOU NEVER REPAY?

You're not actually required to repay policy loans during your lifetime, and some people make a deliberate choice not to. If you go that route, here's what happens:

- Interest continues to compound against the loan balance year after year
- The outstanding balance (principal plus interest) reduces your death benefit
- If the loan balance grows to exceed the cash value, the policy can lapse
- A lapse with outstanding loans can trigger taxable income

For some people, never repaying is an intentional strategy. They're effectively converting death benefit into lifetime liquidity, which is a legitimate choice if you've thought through and planned for the estate implications.

For most people implementing Infinite Banking, though, the goal is to maintain the policy's health through periodic repayment while using loans tactically when the need arises. You want that borrowing capacity available for future needs, which means keeping loan balances manageable relative to your cash value over the long haul.

MANAGING LAPSE RISK

All of this talk about repayment flexibility might make it sound like you can let loans ride indefinitely without consequence. You can't. A policy lapses when it can no longer sustain itself, and for a policy with outstanding loans, this happens when the loan balance plus accrued interest exceeds the available cash value. Understanding and managing this risk is essential if you're going to borrow against your policy with any regularity.

WHAT CAUSES LAPSE:

Lapse typically results from some combination of factors working against you at the same time:

- Large outstanding loans relative to cash value
- Interest compounding over many years without repayment
- Missed premium payments reducing cash value growth
- Lower-than-expected dividends reducing the cushion you thought you had

WHY LAPSE IS BAD:

If your policy lapses while you have an outstanding loan, the IRS treats the excess of the loan over your premium basis as taxable income. What this means in practical terms is that you could owe taxes on money you borrowed and spent years ago.

To put some numbers on this: let's say you paid $100,000 in total premiums over the years, which becomes your basis. You borrowed $80,000 at some point, and that balance grew to $120,000 with accumulated interest. Then the policy lapses. You now have $20,000 of taxable income, calculated as the $120,000 loan minus your $100,000 basis.

Beyond the tax hit, a lapse means losing your death benefit and your entire liquidity infrastructure. The policy that was supposed to provide financial flexibility instead creates a tax problem and then simply disappears from your financial life.

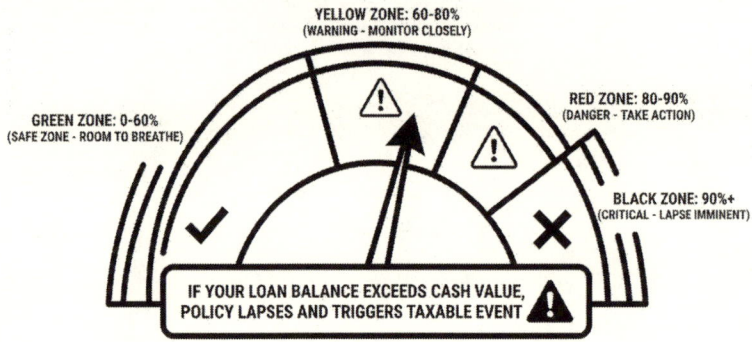

HOW TO PREVENT LAPSE:

The good news is that lapse is entirely preventable if you stay on top of things. Start by monitoring your loan-to-cash-value ratio on a regular basis. A common guideline is keeping loans below 70-80% of cash value to maintain a reasonable safety margin, and some advisors recommend even more conservative limits than that.

Make sure you're paying at least the annual interest on any loans you have outstanding. This single habit prevents the balance from compounding against you and eating into your cushion over time.

Keep up with your premium payments as well. Skipping premiums might save cash in the short term, but it reduces the cash value growth that supports your loans, which can put you in a tighter spot down the road. Pay attention to dividend credits too. If dividends decline significantly from what you were expecting, your cash value grows more slowly, and this reduces the cushion supporting your loans in ways that might not be immediately obvious.

Finally, request annual in-force illustrations that show your current loan balance, cash value, and projections under different scenarios. Don't assume things are fine just because you haven't heard otherwise. Verify the numbers yourself so you're never caught off guard.

WHAT TO DO IF LAPSE IS LOOMING:

If your loan balance is approaching dangerous territory, you still have some options available to you:

- Make principal payments to reduce the loan balance directly
- Make additional premium payments to increase cash value
- Reduce or eliminate future borrowing until the ratio improves
- Consider partial surrender of PUAs if that option is available in your policy

Some policies offer overloan protection riders that prevent lapse in certain circumstances, so if you plan to borrow aggressively over the life of your policy, this rider may be worth the additional cost for the peace of mind it provides. The goal with all of this is never reaching the point where lapse becomes a real threat in the first place. Active monitoring combined with periodic repayment is what keeps the policy healthy and working for you over the long haul.

THE INSURANCE COMPANY AS COUNTERPARTY

At this point, it's worth stepping back and thinking about who's on the other side of this arrangement. When you implement this strategy, you're entering a long-term relationship with an insurance company, and understanding what that means helps you evaluate the whole thing realistically.

WHAT YOU'RE TRUSTING THEM TO DO:

You're trusting them to honor the contract terms for decades. The guaranteed interest rate, the loan provisions, the death benefit calculations are all specified in the contract, and you're counting on the company to honor those commitments for potentially 50+ years.

You're also trusting them to remain solvent. An insurance company that fails can't pay claims or honor policy provisions, and while insurance companies are heavily regulated with policyholder claims having priority in insolvency, company failure would still disrupt your strategy significantly.

Beyond that, you're trusting them to process loans efficiently. The tactical value of policy loans depends entirely on getting funds when you need them, so a company that takes weeks to process loan requests undermines the flexibility that makes the strategy work in the first place.

And finally, you're trusting them to maintain reasonable dividend rates. While dividends aren't guaranteed, you're counting on the company to manage its business competently and share surplus with policyholders fairly over time.

HOW THIS COMPARES TO OTHER COUNTERPARTIES:

Every financial relationship involves counterparty risk, so it's worth thinking about how insurance companies stack up against the alternatives.

Banks can freeze accounts, change terms, call loans, or fail (though deposits are insured up to certain limits). Crypto exchanges can be hacked, freeze withdrawals, or collapse entirely, as we've seen happen repeatedly over the past few years. DeFi protocols can have bugs, be exploited, or face governance attacks that wipe out user funds.

Insurance companies, while certainly not risk-free, operate under heavy regulation, maintain substantial reserves, and have long track records of honoring their commitments. The oldest mutual insurers have paid dividends and claims for over 150 years through world wars, depressions, and financial crises, which gives you some sense of their institutional durability.

State guaranty associations also provide a backstop if an insurer fails. Coverage limits vary by state, typically ranging from $300,000-$500,000 per policy. This isn't quite the same as FDIC insurance, but it does provide meaningful protection if something goes wrong.

DUE DILIGENCE ON YOUR COUNTERPARTY:

Before committing to a carrier, make sure you verify:

- Financial strength ratings from multiple agencies
- Regulatory standing in your state
- History of honoring policy provisions
- Reputation for loan processing speed and service
- Guaranty association coverage in your state

You're not eliminating counterparty risk this way, but you are choosing a counterparty with a long track record, heavy regulation, and alignment of interests (since mutual companies are owned by their policyholders).

For someone who chose crypto partly to avoid counterparty risk with traditional financial institutions, this might require some philosophical reconciliation. The policy doesn't give you the same sovereignty as self-custody crypto, and I want to be upfront about that. What it does provide is something self-custody simply can't deliver: stable liquidity that doesn't depend on market conditions or your willingness to sell.

The way we think about it is that these two approaches actually complement each other quite well. You use self-custody for assets you want to hold with maximum sovereignty, and you use insurance for the liquidity infrastructure that lets you maintain that sovereignty by never being forced to sell at the wrong time.

INTEREST RATE SENSITIVITY AND LOAN COSTS

Beyond the counterparty relationship, there's another external factor that affects how your policy performs over time. Interest rates affect both sides of your policy: what you earn on cash value and what you pay on loans. Understanding this sensitivity helps you plan for different environments and make better borrowing decisions.

HOW RATES AFFECT CASH VALUE GROWTH:

Insurance companies invest primarily in bonds and other fixed-income securities, which means when interest rates are high, those investments earn more, and that supports higher dividend crediting rates. When rates are low, investment returns decline, which puts pressure on dividends across the board.

The general decline in interest rates from the 1980s through 2020 corresponded with declining dividend rates across the entire industry. A policy that credited 10% back in 1990 might only credit 5% today. This doesn't mean the strategy doesn't work anymore. What it means is that projections from decades ago overstated what actually happened, and you should keep that in mind when looking at historical examples.

More recently, rising rates could support higher future dividends, which would be a welcome change. But insurance companies tend to be conservative about these things, and dividend increases typically lag rate increases by several years as the company's investment portfolio gradually turns over.

HOW RATES AFFECT LOAN COSTS:

Policy loan rates vary depending on how your contract is structured:

Fixed rate loans have a rate specified in the contract, often somewhere in the 5-8% range. This rate doesn't change regardless of what's happening in the broader market, which means you know exactly what your borrowing costs will be from day one.

Variable rate loans are tied to some index or to the company's crediting rate. These can be lower than fixed rates when market rates are low, but they can also increase if rates rise, which adds some uncertainty to your planning.

In a rising rate environment, fixed-rate loans become more attractive because you're locking in a borrowing cost while your cash value crediting might be increasing. In a falling rate environment, variable-rate loans might end up being cheaper, though your cash value growth also slows down at the same time.

THE SPREAD MATTERS:

What really matters most when you're evaluating borrowing decisions is the spread between what you earn and what you pay. If your policy credits 5% and loans cost 6%, the net cost of borrowing is roughly 1%, which is quite manageable. If your policy credits 4% and loans cost 8%, you're looking at a net cost of 4%, which changes the math considerably.

It's worth remembering that non-direct recognition policies maintain the full crediting rate even when you have loans outstanding, while direct recognition policies reduce your crediting when you borrow. This difference affects the effective spread significantly and is another reason why the recognition method matters so much for active borrowers.

Before you borrow, take the time to calculate the effective cost by asking yourself:

- What's the loan interest rate?
- What's the current crediting rate on cash value?
- Does the recognition method affect crediting while I have loans outstanding?
- What's the net spread between these numbers?

Once you have that figured out, compare the net cost to your alternatives: the tax cost of selling crypto, the interest rate on other borrowing options you might have access to, or the opportunity cost of not pursuing whatever you need the funds for. That comparison is what should drive your decision about whether a policy loan makes sense in any given situation.

TAX CONSIDERATIONS SPECIFIC TO CRYPTO INVESTORS

Beyond interest rate sensitivity, taxes are another factor you need to think through carefully. The good news is that the tax treatment of policy loans is straightforward: they're not taxable events. But crypto investors face some specific tax considerations worth understanding, so here's what you need to consider:

FUNDING PREMIUMS WITH CRYPTO PROCEEDS:

If you sell crypto to generate cash for premium payments, that sale is a taxable event, which means you'll owe capital gains tax on any appreciation.

Now, this doesn't eliminate the tax benefit of the policy. What it does is sequence things differently. You pay capital gains now on the crypto sale, then the policy grows tax-deferred from that point forward, and future loans against the policy remain tax-free.

For someone who's planning to take profits anyway, routing those proceeds to a policy rather than letting them sit in a bank account puts that capital to work building future liquidity instead of just earning minimal interest.

TRACKING COST BASIS:

Your policy's cost basis is the total after-tax premiums you've paid over the years. This basis becomes important if you ever surrender the policy or if it lapses with a loan outstanding.

Make sure you keep careful records of:

- All premium payments (both base premium and PUAs)
- The source of funds for each payment
- Any loans taken and repaid
- Interest paid on loans

Your insurance company will track some of this information, but maintaining your own records ensures accuracy and helps considerably with tax planning down the road.

STATE TAX CONSIDERATIONS:

State tax treatment of life insurance varies more than you might expect. Some states follow federal treatment exactly, while others have different rules for:

- Deductibility of premium payments (which are generally not deductible anywhere)
- Treatment of policy loans
- Treatment of death benefits
- Estate tax implications

If you live in a high-tax state or have moved between states during the life of your policy, it's worth verifying the treatment with a tax professional who's familiar with both life insurance and your specific state's rules.

COORDINATING WITH CRYPTO TAX PLANNING:

Policy loans can actually become part of a broader tax planning strategy in some pretty useful ways.

Instead of selling crypto to fund a large purchase and triggering gains all at once, you can take a policy loan instead. This lets you spread your crypto sales over multiple years to manage bracket exposure, using the policy loan to bridge the timing gap between when you need cash and when it's actually tax-efficient to realize gains.

Here's an example of how this might work in practice: let's say you want to buy a $200,000 property. Selling $200,000 of crypto this year would push you into a higher tax bracket and create a substantial tax bill. Instead, you could:

- Take a $200,000 policy loan now to make the purchase
- Sell $50,000 of crypto this year to begin repayment
- Sell $50,000 each of the next three years

COORDINATING WITH YOUR CRYPTO HOLDINGS | 91

- Spread the gain recognition over four years at lower rates

The policy loan provides immediate liquidity while you manage the tax recognition strategically over time rather than taking the full hit in a single year.

WORKING WITH PROFESSIONALS:

The intersection of crypto taxation and life insurance taxation is complex enough that professional guidance is genuinely valuable here. When you're looking for help, try to find a CPA who understands:

- Cryptocurrency tax treatment
- Life insurance tax treatment
- Your specific state's rules
- How all the pieces fit together in your particular situation

The money spent on good tax advice often pays for itself many times over through avoided mistakes or optimized strategies, so this is one area where I'd encourage you not to cut corners.

THE EXECUTION PROTOCOL

Now that you understand the mechanics and the reasoning behind them, it's time to talk about what this actually looks like in practice. The concepts are important, but they don't mean much until you actually put them to work, so we'll take a look at how the implementation goes:

STEP 1: ASSESS YOUR READINESS

Before anything else, you need to honestly evaluate whether you're actually ready for this:

- Do you have stable income to sustain premium payments for 5+ years?

- Do you have crypto holdings you're committed to holding long-term?
- Do you have capital beyond immediate needs and emergency reserves?
- Are you patient enough to wait 3-5 years before meaningful borrowing capacity develops?

If any of those answers is no, my advice is to wait until your situation changes. Jumping into this prematurely just wastes money and creates frustration, and there's no prize for starting before you're ready.

STEP 2: DEFINE YOUR OBJECTIVES

Once you've confirmed you're ready, get specific about what you're actually trying to accomplish:

- What liquidity needs do you anticipate down the road? Think about tax bills, down payments, investment opportunities, emergencies.
- What dollar amount of borrowing capacity do you want to build, and by when do you need it?
- How much can you realistically commit to annual premiums without creating financial strain?
- What's your timeline here? Are you building for needs five years out or twenty?

The answers to these questions will shape all of your policy design decisions, so it's worth spending some real time thinking them through before you talk to anyone about buying a policy.

STEP 3: FIND THE RIGHT ADVISOR

This step matters more than most people realize. Interview multiple advisors using the questions from Chapter 22, and look for:

- Experience with Infinite Banking specifically
- Understanding of crypto investor needs
- Willingness to show multiple carrier options
- Ability to explain MEC implications clearly
- No pressure tactics or rushing you toward a decision

Take your time with this process, because the wrong advisor almost inevitably leads to the wrong policy design, and you'll be living with that mistake for a long time.

STEP 4: EVALUATE CARRIERS AND POLICY DESIGNS

With your advisor's help, compare options from multiple carriers:

- Run illustrations side by side so you can see the differences clearly
- Compare cash value trajectories under both guaranteed and illustrated scenarios
- Verify loan provisions and recognition methods for each option
- Check dividend history and financial strength ratings
- Calculate MEC limits and maximum funding capacity

Whatever you do, don't rush this step. The policy you choose will be with you for decades, so the extra time you invest here pays dividends for the rest of your life.

STEP 5: APPLY FOR COVERAGE

The application process involves several components:

- Detailed health questions and possibly a medical exam
- Financial documentation for larger policies
- Source of funds documentation
- Underwriting review by the insurance company

The whole process typically takes somewhere between 4-8 weeks, and it's worth knowing upfront that approval isn't guaranteed. Health issues or other factors can affect your rating or even result in a decline, so don't count on the policy being in place until you actually have it.

STEP 6: ESTABLISH YOUR FUNDING RHYTHM

Once the policy is issued and you're ready to go:

- Set up automatic premium payments to ensure you never miss one
- Decide your PUA contribution strategy for the first year
- Create a calendar reminder to review annual statements
- Document your funding plan and the rationale behind it so you remember why you made the choices you did

STEP 7: MONITOR AND ADJUST

Ongoing management is an essential part of making this work over the long haul, and it includes:

- Annual review of your in-force illustration
- Tracking cash value growth against the original projections
- Monitoring your loan-to-cash-value ratio if you're borrowing

- Adjusting PUA contributions based on your circumstances each year
- Verifying that the policy continues to align with your goals as they evolve

The important thing to understand is that this policy isn't something you can just set and forget. Active management is what ensures it continues serving your purposes the way you intended.

STEP 8: USE LOANS STRATEGICALLY

When the time comes to actually borrow against your policy:

- Request the loan from your insurance company
- Receive the funds, which typically arrive within days
- Deploy the capital wherever you need it
- Establish a repayment intention, even if the timeline is flexible
- Track the loan balance and interest accrual so nothing surprises you

STEP 9: REPLENISH AND REPEAT

After using a loan, the cycle continues:

- Repay according to your predetermined triggers and your actual cash flow
- Continue your premium funding to rebuild borrowing capacity
- Prepare for the next time you need to tap the system

What you'll find is that the system becomes more powerful over time as cash value compounds and your comfort with the mechanics increases. The first loan might feel a little uncertain, but by the third or fourth time you've been through the cycle, it becomes second nature.

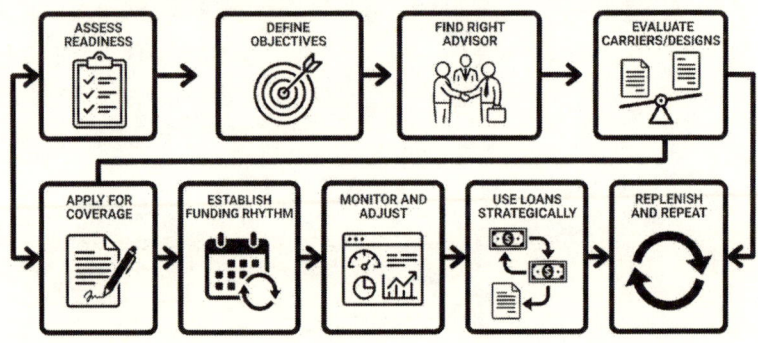

BUILDING YOUR ALLOCATION FRAMEWORK

Beyond the mechanics of getting a policy in place, you need to think about how it fits within your broader financial picture. Here's a framework for thinking about allocation:

The three-bucket model:

Bucket 1 - Liquid reserves: This is cash or cash equivalents for immediate needs. You want three to six months of expenses at minimum here, and this money needs to be accessible within days without fluctuating in value. Think of it as your financial shock absorber for the unexpected stuff that life throws at you.

Bucket 2 - Policy cash value: This is your borrowable capital for larger needs and opportunities. It takes years to build, but once it's there, it provides tax-advantaged liquidity you can tap whenever you need it. As a general target, aim for somewhere in the range of 20-40% of the amount you want available for potential borrowing needs.

Bucket 3 - Crypto holdings: This is your growth allocation. We're talking high volatility with high potential upside, self-custodied, and ideally not touched for liquidity needs except in truly extreme circumstances.

Each bucket serves a distinct purpose in your overall financial architecture:

- Bucket 1 handles your day-to-day fluctuations and provides liquidity for small emergencies

- Bucket 2 handles your significant needs without forcing you to sell Bucket 3

- Bucket 3 serves to capture the long-term growth potential while you sleep

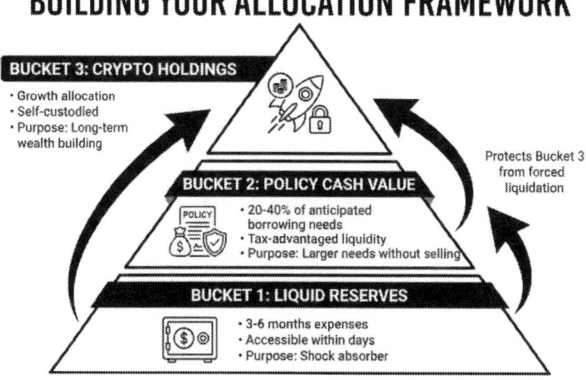

SIZING THE POLICY:

The way to think about this is to work backward from your anticipated borrowing needs. Let's say you might need to access $200,000 over the next decade for various purposes like taxes, investment opportunities, or major purchases. That means you want cash value that can support that level of borrowing comfortably.

Given that you can typically borrow 80-90% of your cash value, you'd want somewhere in the range of $220,000-$250,000 in cash value to support $200,000 in potential borrowing.

To reach that level in 7-10 years requires annual premiums in the $20,000-$30,000 range, depending on policy design and how performance plays out over time.

Now, these numbers are just illustrative to show you how the math works. Your situation will differ based on your age, health class, carrier choice, and the specific design decisions you make. But the underlying logic works the same way regardless: define the borrowing capacity you want to have available, then work backward to figure out the premium funding required to get there.

BALANCING ALLOCATION OVER TIME:

Early in the strategy, most of your wealth will remain in crypto while the policy builds its foundation. This is completely normal and expected, since the policy takes years to become meaningfully useful for borrowing purposes.

As years pass and cash value accumulates, the policy starts to represent a larger share of your total financial picture. What this gives you is increasing stability and optionality that you simply didn't have before.

Some people eventually hold substantial portions of their wealth in policy cash value because they come to value that stability. Others maintain it as a smaller allocation focused specifically on providing liquidity when needed. Your particular balance depends on your goals, your risk tolerance, and how the strategy performs for you over time.

AVOIDING OVER-ALLOCATION:

The policy shouldn't consume capital you need for other purposes, and it's important to watch for warning signs that you might be over-allocating:

- Premium payments are causing financial stress
- You're neglecting emergency reserves to fund premiums
- You're passing on investment opportunities because too much capital is locked in premiums
- You're considering surrendering the policy or taking loans just to cover routine expenses

If you find yourself in any of these situations, the right move is to reduce your premium funding (particularly PUA contributions) until your situation stabilizes. A sustainable strategy that you can maintain for decades beats an over-ambitious one that falls apart after a few years because you stretched too thin.

INFINITE BANKING FOR CRYPTO INVESTORS

THINKING IN DECADES

Towards the front of this book, we talked a bit about the skepticism surrounding this strategy. Now that you've got a lot more context, it's worth revisiting some of the common objections you'll encounter from smart people who question Infinite Banking. Some of their concerns are valid and deserve a thoughtful response, while others simply miss the point of what we're trying to accomplish here. Knowing the difference helps you evaluate the strategy honestly and respond to critics effectively.

OBJECTION: "WHOLE LIFE INSURANCE IS A BAD INVESTMENT."

This is actually true. Whole life insurance is a bad investment. It's also completely irrelevant to what we're doing here.

The strategy doesn't use whole life insurance as an investment. It uses whole life insurance as a liquidity tool. The returns on cash value are modest compared to equities or crypto, but that's not the point at all. The point is having stable, accessible capital that doesn't require selling volatile assets or asking permission from banks.

Comparing whole life returns to stock market returns is like comparing the return on your checking account to the return on your brokerage account. Your checking account earns almost nothing, but that doesn't make it useless. It serves a completely different purpose in your financial life.

The relevant comparison isn't "whole life vs. crypto returns." The relevant comparison is "the cost of policy loans vs. the cost of selling crypto when you need liquidity." When you frame it correctly, the math often favors the policy by a wide margin.

OBJECTION: "THE FEES ARE TOO HIGH."

Fees exist. Commissions are front-loaded. The early years show negative returns relative to premiums paid. All of that is true.

The real question is whether the fees are worth what you get in return. And what you get is:

- Tax-advantaged growth
- Tax-free access to capital
- No credit checks or approval processes
- No liquidation risk
- Flexible repayment terms
- A stable asset uncorrelated with crypto markets

For someone who would otherwise sell crypto at the wrong time, pay capital gains taxes, and lose future upside, the policy fees are trivial compared to the costs you're avoiding.

Now, the fees matter most for people who don't actually need the liquidity features. If you have ample cash reserves and no anticipated need for policy loans, then yes, you're paying fees for features you won't use. The strategy fits specific circumstances, and it's not designed for everyone.

OBJECTION:
"YOU COULD INVEST THE PREMIUM DIFFERENCE AND COME OUT AHEAD."

The "buy term and invest the difference" argument has been around for decades. The logic goes like this: term insurance is cheaper than whole life, so you should buy term and invest the premium savings in the market. You'll end up with more money.

In isolation, this math often works out. If you consistently invest the difference and achieve market returns, you might accumulate more than the cash value of a whole life policy.

But the argument completely ignores why you might want whole life in the first place. It ignores:

- The tax treatment of policy loans vs. taxable investment withdrawals
- The behavioral reality that most people don't actually invest the difference consistently
- The liquidity characteristics during market stress
- The specific problem of forced selling that crypto investors face

For someone who would actually invest the difference consistently for decades and never need tax-advantaged liquidity, buy term and invest the difference might be the right choice. But for someone who needs a stable borrowing facility that doesn't depend on market conditions, you're comparing apples to oranges.

INFINITE BANKING FOR CRYPTO INVESTORS

OBJECTION:
"INSURANCE COMPANIES ARE JUST ANOTHER INSTITUTION YOU HAVE TO TRUST."

This is a legitimate concern, especially for someone who values the sovereignty that comes with self-custody crypto. You're absolutely trusting the insurance company to honor the contract, remain solvent, and process loans efficiently.

The counterargument isn't that insurance companies are trustless, because they're not. The counterargument is that every financial tool involves tradeoffs, and the question becomes which tradeoffs you're willing to accept for what you're trying to accomplish.

Self-custody crypto gives you maximum sovereignty over those specific assets, but it doesn't give you liquidity without selling. It doesn't give you tax-advantaged growth. It doesn't give you a stable asset class uncorrelated with crypto.

The policy doesn't replace self-custody. It complements it. You maintain maximum sovereignty over your crypto by never being forced to sell, and the policy is what enables that sovereignty to persist through volatility.

Think of it as accepting a small amount of institutional dependency (the insurance company) to preserve a large amount of sovereignty (your crypto holdings). The tradeoff may or may not make sense for your particular situation, but it's not an obvious mistake when you think it through.

OBJECTION:
"DIVIDENDS AREN'T GUARANTEED AND HAVE BEEN DECLINING."

True on both counts. Dividends are not guaranteed, and dividend rates have generally declined over the past few decades as interest rates fell.

This is exactly why you should:

- Evaluate policies based on guaranteed values, not just illustrated values
- Choose carriers with long track records of paying dividends through various conditions
- Use conservative assumptions when projecting future performance
- Understand that the strategy works even with lower dividends, despite slower growth

A policy that credits 4% instead of 6% still provides tax-advantaged growth and tax-free loans. The timeline to build meaningful cash value extends, but the underlying mechanics still work the way they're supposed to.

It's also worth noting that the declining dividend trend isn't guaranteed to continue forever. Rising interest rates could support higher future dividends. But don't count on it. Plan for conservative scenarios and be pleasantly surprised if reality turns out better than expected.

OBJECTION:
"THIS IS TOO COMPLICATED."

Compared to buying crypto and holding it, yes, this is more complicated. There are contracts to understand, designs to evaluate, advisors to vet, and require ongoing management.

The real question is whether the complexity is worth the benefit you're getting. If you have significant crypto holdings and anticipate needing liquidity at some point, the complexity of this strategy is probably less than the complexity of managing forced sales, tax optimization, and alternative borrowing arrangements when you're under pressure.

What we've found is that the strategy becomes much simpler once it's actually implemented. You fund the policy regularly. You monitor it annually. You take loans when needed. You repay when appropriate. The initial setup requires real effort to get right, but the ongoing operation becomes pretty straightforward once you've got the foundation in place.

WHAT CRYPTO AND INSURANCE ACTUALLY SHARE

At first glance, whole life insurance and cryptocurrency seem like they belong to completely different universes. One is a 200-year-old financial instrument sold by suit-wearing agents at wood-paneled offices. The other is a decade-old technology built by cypherpunks who wanted to escape institutional finance entirely.

But when you dig into the philosophical foundations, they actually align more than they differ.

BOTH PRIORITIZE INDIVIDUAL CONTROL

Crypto gives you custody of your assets, and in a truly decentralized network, you're the one who controls what happens to your wealth.

A properly structured whole life policy gives you similar control over your liquidity. No bank approves your loan. No credit committee evaluates your worthiness. If you have cash value, you can access it. The control is contractual rather than cryptographic, but the underlying principle remains the same. You're not asking anyone for permission to use your own money.

BOTH REWARD LONG-TERM THINKING

Crypto rewards those who can hold through volatility, and the gains tend to go to people with conviction who don't panic sell during drawdowns. Short-term traders mostly lose to fees, taxes, and bad timing, while the patient ones accumulate.

Whole life insurance rewards patience even more explicitly. The early years are unfavorable by design, and the strategy only works if you maintain it for decades. The impatient lose to surrender charges and opportunity cost, while those who stick with it end up building substantial resources over time.

BOTH REPRESENT DISTRUST OF TRADITIONAL FINANCE

Crypto emerged from dissatisfaction with central banking, fiat currency debasement, and institutional control over money. The whole premise is that you shouldn't have to trust banks with your financial future.

INFINITE BANKING FOR CRYPTO INVESTORS

Infinite Banking emerged from Nelson Nash's frustration with paying interest to banks for the privilege of using his own money. The whole premise is that you can become your own banker instead of enriching financial institutions every time you need capital.

The specific mechanisms differ quite a bit, but the underlying impulse driving both movements is remarkably similar: create alternatives to institutional dependence.

BOTH REQUIRE EDUCATION AND SELF-RELIANCE

Crypto demands that you understand custody, private keys, security practices, and market dynamics. The ecosystem doesn't protect you from your own mistakes, which means you have to know what you're doing or you'll get burned.

Infinite Banking demands that you understand policy mechanics, design principles, carrier selection, and loan management. The insurance industry will happily sell you a poorly designed product if you don't know better, which means you have to know what you're doing here too.

Both spaces have information asymmetries that favor the educated participant. Both punish ignorance. Both reward those who invest the time to understand how things actually work under the hood.

Crypto provides growth potential and true ownership of digital assets. Insurance provides stability and liquidity infrastructure. When you put them together, they create something neither can deliver on its own: the ability to maintain high-conviction positions through any market condition without ever being forced to sell.

The crypto gives you the upside. The policy gives you the ability to actually capture that upside by staying invested through the brutal volatility. Each component makes the other more valuable in ways that aren't obvious until you see them working together.

This isn't about abandoning crypto principles in favor of traditional finance. It's about using whatever tools serve your goals, regardless of which world they come from. True sovereignty means making your own choices based on what actually works for your situation. And sometimes those choices include instruments you didn't initially consider.

PLANNING ACROSS LIFE STAGES

The strategy plays out over decades, which means how you implement it should evolve as your life circumstances change.

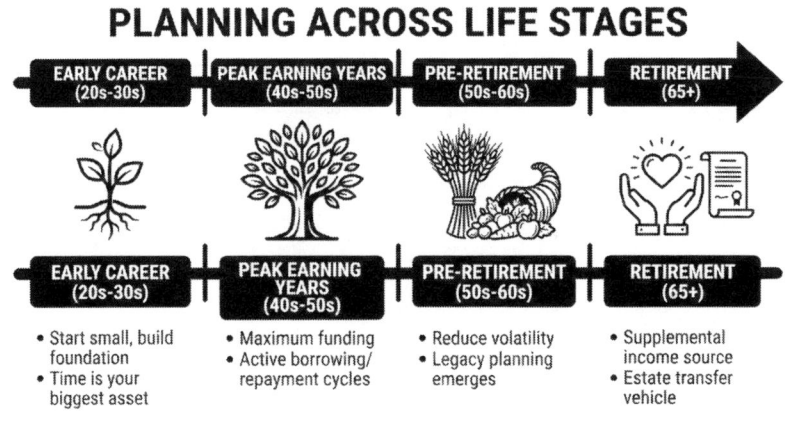

EARLY CAREER (20s-30s):

If you're young with limited capital but growing income, the smart move is to start small:

- Begin with premiums you can sustain even if income fluctuates
- Prioritize building the policy foundation over maximizing early cash value

- Focus on consistency rather than aggressive funding
- Use term insurance for any death benefit needs beyond what the whole life provides
- Let time work in your favor through compounding

The biggest advantage of starting young is simply time. Even modest premiums compound into substantial cash value over 30-40 years, and the policy you start at 28 will be far more powerful by 50 than one started at 45.

The risk at this stage is overcommitting before you really know what your financial life will look like. Don't lock into premiums that will strain you if income drops or other priorities emerge. Start conservatively and then increase as your situation stabilizes over time.

PEAK EARNING YEARS (40s-50s):

This is typically when the strategy becomes most active:

- Income is higher, supporting larger premium contributions
- Liquidity needs are greater (education costs, property, business opportunities)
- Cash value has built to useful levels
- Active borrowing and repayment cycles begin

This stage often involves the most coordination between your policy and your crypto holdings. You might take loans to avoid selling crypto during accumulation phases, then repay those loans from crypto profits during bull markets. You could use policy liquidity to fund opportunities that would otherwise require selling, or maximize PUA contributions during high-income years when you have excess cash flow.

The key risk during this period is over-borrowing. With substantial cash value available, the temptation is to tap it frequently for all kinds of things. Maintain discipline around loan-to-cash-value ratios and repayment intentions, because it's easy to let balances creep up without realizing how exposed you've become.

PRE-RETIREMENT (50s-60s):

As you approach retirement, your priorities naturally shift:

- Reducing volatility becomes more important
- Legacy planning considerations emerge
- The policy's death benefit becomes more relevant
- Loan activity might decrease as you preserve rather than deploy capital

This stage often involves making sure your policy loans are manageable relative to cash value, along with considering whether to pay down loans before retirement kicks in. You'll also want to evaluate the death benefit in the context of your broader estate plans, and you might consider reducing your crypto allocation in favor of stable assets including policy cash value.

RETIREMENT AND BEYOND (65+):

In retirement, the policy serves different purposes than it did during your working years:

- Source of supplemental income through systematic loans if needed
- Estate transfer vehicle through the death benefit

- Tax-advantaged asset for legacy planning
- Stable asset uncorrelated with market volatility

The considerations at this stage include managing loans so they don't threaten policy lapse, coordinating the death benefit with your overall estate plans, potentially gifting or transferring policy ownership to the next generation, and using the policy strategically for required minimum distribution planning.

ADAPTING TO INCOME CHANGES

Life stages are one thing, but income is its own beast entirely. Jobs change, businesses have good years and bad years, and crypto income is notoriously volatile. The strategy must accommodate these realities, which means you need to think through how you'll handle both the ups and the downs.

WHEN INCOME INCREASES:

More income creates opportunities to accelerate the strategy in meaningful ways:

- Increase PUA contributions up to MEC limits
- Fund additional policies if one is insufficient for your needs
- Build cash value faster so you reach borrowing capacity sooner

The temptation when your income jumps is to increase lifestyle spending proportionally, which is completely understandable.

But directing some of those income increases to the policy instead builds long-term optionality without any obvious sacrifice to your current quality of life.

WHEN INCOME DECREASES:

Reduced income requires prioritization and some tough choices:

- Maintain base premium payments if at all possible
- Reduce or eliminate PUA contributions
- Avoid taking new loans that will strain your repayment capacity
- Consider paying interest-only on existing loans to prevent the balance from compounding against you

Most policies have grace periods for missed premiums, typically somewhere around 30-31 days. If you absolutely must miss a payment, make sure you catch up during the grace period to avoid any negative consequences to your policy.

Some policies also allow automatic premium loans, which means they'll use your cash value to pay premiums if you don't pay out of pocket. This keeps the policy in force, but it also increases your loan balance and reduces your cash value at the same time. Think of it as a safety valve for emergencies rather than a long-term solution.

HANDLING IRREGULAR CRYPTO INCOME:

Crypto income is particularly lumpy compared to traditional income sources. You might have years with substantial realized gains and high income, followed by years with losses and minimal income. You could experience sudden liquidity events from token sales or exits, or go through extended periods of accumulation where you have no realized income at all.

The key is structuring your policy funding to handle this variability:

- Set your base premium at a level you can sustain even in your lowest-income years
- Use PUA capacity to absorb windfalls during high-income years
- Maintain cash reserves specifically for the purpose of covering premiums during dry spells
- Consider funding premiums from stablecoin reserves rather than forcing fresh sales at inopportune times

The flexibility of PUA contributions is particularly valuable when your income is irregular. You're not locked into a specific amount each year, which means you can contribute more when you have excess capital and scale back when things are tighter.

IF YOU CAN'T MAINTAIN THE POLICY:

Sometimes circumstances make continuing the policy impossible, and if you reach that point, it's important to understand what options are available to you:

- **Reduced paid-up option:** You stop paying premiums entirely and convert to a smaller, fully paid-up policy. No more premiums are required going forward, but your death benefit and future cash value growth are both reduced.

- **Extended term option:** This converts your cash value to term insurance for a specified period. Coverage continues until the term expires, but no cash value accumulates during that time.

- **Surrender:** You take the cash surrender value (which is your cash value minus any surrender charges) and walk away from the policy entirely. Be aware that this triggers taxable income on any gains inside the policy.

- **1035 exchange:** This allows you to transfer to a different policy, perhaps one with lower premiums that better fits your current situation, without triggering any taxes.

Before you surrender a policy, we'd strongly encourage you to explore all the alternatives first. Years of premium payments and compounding are permanently lost when you surrender, and even a reduced paid-up policy preserves some value from everything you've invested up to that point.

ESTATE PLANNING CONSIDERATIONS

Up to this point, we've been focused on liquidity and lifetime benefits. But there's a reason it's called life insurance, and the death benefit makes this an estate planning tool as well. How you structure ownership and beneficiaries affects what happens when you die, so it's worth understanding the options.

BASIC DEATH BENEFIT MECHANICS:

When you die, the insurance company pays the death benefit to your named beneficiaries. If you have outstanding policy loans at that point, the loan balance plus accrued interest gets subtracted from the death benefit first.

To put some numbers on this:

- **Death benefit:** $500,000
- **Outstanding loans:** $150,000
- **Net to beneficiaries:** $350,000

The death benefit is generally income tax-free to beneficiaries, which makes it one of the most favorable tax treatments of any wealth transfer vehicle available.

OWNERSHIP STRUCTURES:

Personal ownership: You own the policy directly. This is the simplest approach, but the death benefit gets included in your taxable estate for estate tax purposes.

Irrevocable Life Insurance Trust (ILIT): The trust owns the policy, which means death benefits go to the trust rather than your estate. When structured properly, this removes the death benefit from your taxable estate entirely.

The ILIT approach makes the most sense for larger estates where estate taxes are a real concern. It does add complexity and cost to the arrangement, but it can save substantial estate taxes for high-net-worth individuals.

Spousal ownership: Your spouse owns the policy on your life, so death benefits go directly to your spouse. The unlimited marital deduction means there's no estate tax on transfer to a surviving spouse. This is simpler than setting up an ILIT, though it provides less control and doesn't actually remove assets from the combined estate.

COORDINATING WITH CRYPTO HOLDINGS:

Your crypto holdings face a different estate challenge that's worth thinking about: access. If your heirs can't get into your wallets, the crypto is effectively lost forever.

The policy can actually help with this situation in several ways:

- The death benefit provides immediate liquidity to heirs while crypto access is being sorted out
- Your heirs have cash to pay estate taxes and expenses without being forced to sell crypto under pressure

- The stable asset provides financial security while volatile crypto holdings are being transferred

Make sure you document your crypto access clearly. Keep seed phrases, hardware wallet instructions, and account information somewhere your executor or trusted contacts can actually find and access. The policy provides the financial cushion that gives everyone breathing room while these details are being handled.

USING DEATH BENEFIT FOR EQUALIZATION:

If you have multiple heirs and illiquid assets like crypto or a business, the death benefit can help equalize inheritances in a way that makes sense for everyone.

Here's an example of how this might work:

- Your estate includes $2 million in crypto and a $1 million business
- You have two children, one involved in the business and one not
- You leave the business to the involved child
- You leave the crypto plus the death benefit to the uninvolved child to equalize things

This method avoids forcing the sale of assets just to create equal distributions, and it lets each heir receive the assets that are most appropriate for their situation.

LOANS AND ESTATE PLANNING:

Outstanding policy loans reduce the death benefit, which means if your estate plan depends on a specific death benefit amount, loan management becomes an estate planning consideration you need to think through.

You might commit to paying down loans before you reach a certain age, or you could maintain loans below a threshold that preserves your minimum intended death benefit. Alternatively, you might simply accept a reduced death benefit as the price of lifetime liquidity and plan accordingly.

There's no universal right answer here. The appropriate balance depends entirely on your priorities for lifetime access versus legacy transfer, and only you can decide how to weigh those competing considerations.

WHEN THINGS GO WRONG

At this point, you might be feeling pretty good about how all the pieces fit together. But we'd be doing you a disservice if we didn't walk through what can go wrong. No strategy works perfectly in all scenarios, and understanding the potential problems helps you plan for contingencies and recognize warning signs before they become crises.

PROBLEM:
POLICY LAPSES WITH OUTSTANDING LOANS

If your policy lapses while you have loans outstanding, you face a taxable event. The excess of loan balance over your premium basis is treated as taxable income, which can create a nasty surprise at tax time.

This can happen for several reasons:

- Loans plus interest grew faster than cash value
- You stopped paying premiums and cash value depleted
- Dividend cuts reduced the cushion supporting loans

Prevention:

The good news is that this is entirely avoidable if you stay vigilant. Make sure you're monitoring loan-to-cash-value ratios regularly, and commit to paying at least the annual interest on any loans you have outstanding. Even when cash is tight, do everything you can to maintain your premium payments, and always build some buffer into your borrowing so you can absorb dividend variations without getting into trouble.

Recovery if you're approaching trouble:

If you find yourself getting close to dangerous territory, you still have options. You can make extra principal payments to reduce the loan balance directly, or make extra premium payments to increase your cash value. At a minimum, reduce any future borrowing until the ratios improve, and consider a partial surrender of PUAs if that option is available in your policy.

PROBLEM: POLICY UNDERPERFORMS ILLUSTRATIONS

Illustrations show projected performance that may not actually materialize in the real world. If dividends come in lower than illustrated, your cash value grows more slowly than you were expecting. This isn't catastrophic by any means, but it does mean that reaching borrowing capacity takes longer than planned, the cushion supporting your loans is smaller than you thought, and the strategy delivers less than you originally hoped for.

Response:

The best approach here is to increase your premium contributions if possible to compensate for the slower growth. Beyond that, you'll need to adjust your timeline expectations and revisit your borrowing plans to account for the lower capacity. Sometimes you just have to accept a reduced but still functional strategy that gets you most of what you wanted.

PROBLEM: CARRIER FINANCIAL TROUBLE

Insurance companies rarely fail, but it does happen from time to time. If your carrier experiences financial difficulty, you might see dividend payments reduced or eliminated entirely. Loan processing could slow down considerably, and in extreme cases, the company might even be taken over by regulators.

Prevention:

The best protection here is choosing carriers with strong financial ratings from the start, then monitoring those ratings over time to catch any deterioration early. If you have substantial exposure to a single carrier, it's worth considering diversifying across multiple companies to spread your risk.

Recovery if trouble emerges:

Should problems develop with your carrier, consider executing a 1035 exchange to move your policy to a stronger company. In the meantime, reduce your dependence on policy loans while the situation remains uncertain, and keep a close eye on any regulatory proceedings so you understand the implications for your policy.

It's worth noting that state guaranty associations provide a backstop in these situations, typically covering somewhere between $300,000 and $500,000 per policy depending on your state. This offers meaningful protection, though it's not unlimited.

PROBLEM: YOU NEED LIQUIDITY BEFORE CASH VALUE BUILDS

The strategy takes years to develop meaningful borrowing capacity. If you need liquidity before that capacity builds, the policy simply can't help you.

Prevention:

This is exactly why you shouldn't implement the strategy if you have near-term liquidity needs. Make sure you're maintaining separate liquid reserves for shorter-term requirements, and be genuinely realistic about the timeline during your planning process.

Response if you misjudged:

If you find yourself needing money before the policy can provide it, don't try to rely on a young policy for current needs. Instead, find alternative liquidity sources to address the immediate situation while maintaining the policy for future needs. Whatever you do, avoid surrendering an underfunded policy unless you've truly exhausted every other option, because you'll lose years of premium payments and compounding that you can never get back.

PROBLEM:
PERSONAL FINANCIAL CRISIS

Job loss, divorce, health crisis, or other personal emergencies can disrupt any financial plan, and there's only so much any strategy can do to protect you from major life upheavals.

The policy does provide some resilience in difficult times. If you have a waiver of premium rider, it suspends your premium obligation during disability. Policy loans can provide emergency funds when you need them. And the cash surrender value exists as a last resort if nothing else works.

That said, a policy doesn't make you invulnerable to life's curveballs. A severe enough crisis can force difficult choices, including potentially surrendering the policy you've worked so hard to build.

The best protection is maintaining overall financial health across all dimensions of your life. This means keeping adequate emergency reserves that are completely separate from the policy, carrying appropriate insurance coverage for health, disability, and liability, diversifying your income sources where possible, and always borrowing conservatively relative to your actual capacity. When you do all of these things well, you create multiple layers of protection that can absorb shocks without forcing you to unwind your long-term strategy.

RED FLAGS AND WARNING SIGNS

Beyond knowing what can go wrong, part of managing this well over the long haul is knowing how to recognize warning signs before they escalate into real problems. The earlier you catch a problem, the more options you'll have for fixing it. Here's a few red flags to look out for:

Red flags in policy design:

- Illustrated cash value dramatically exceeds guaranteed value (suggests aggressive assumptions)
- PUA capacity is small relative to base premium (limits acceleration potential)
- Loan interest rate is variable without cap (unpredictable borrowing costs)
- Direct recognition reduces dividends when borrowing (penalizes loan usage)
- Agent can't explain MEC implications clearly (doesn't understand the strategy)
- Pressure to decide quickly without time to evaluate (sales tactics over your interests)

Red flags in policy performance:

- Cash value consistently trails illustrated projections (dividends disappointing)
- Loan balance growing faster than cash value (approaching lapse risk)
- Carrier financial ratings declining (company in trouble)

- Significantly lower dividends than peer companies (possible management issues)

Red flags in your own behavior:

- Taking loans for routine expenses rather than strategic purposes (using the policy as a piggy bank)
- Ignoring loan balances and not tracking accumulation (losing awareness of position)
- Skipping premium payments regularly (policy health deteriorating)
- Not reviewing annual statements (missing warning signs)
- Planning to repay loans "eventually" without specific triggers (drifting toward trouble)

WHAT TO DO IF YOU SEE RED FLAGS:

If any of these warning signs show up, the most important thing is to stop and evaluate before taking any additional action. Request updated in-force illustrations that show the current reality of your policy, and consult with your advisor about what the implications are and what options you have available. Take time to consider whether a course correction is possible or whether bigger changes are needed to get things back on track.

Whatever you do, don't ignore problems hoping they'll je resolve themselves. That almost never works, and it usually just makes the eventual reckoning more painful.

Early intervention is always easier than crisis management, and understanding where the danger zones are can help you stay alert. A loan balance approaching 60% of cash value is a warning that deserves your attention. At 80%, the situation becomes urgent and requires immediate action. At 90%, you're in serious trouble and your options are narrowing fast. The key is to address issues when they're still warnings rather than waiting until they've become full-blown emergencies.

THE INFINITE BANKING OPERATING SYSTEM

We've covered a lot of ground together. If you've made it this far, you're not someone who just skims through things hoping to find a shortcut. You're the person who's felt that pit in your stomach when you needed cash and the only option was selling crypto at the worst possible time. Or maybe you haven't been forced to sell yet, but you know the day is coming and you want to be ready.

Either way, you now have something most crypto investors don't: a real solution you can actually build, so let's bring it all together:.

THE CORE PROBLEM:

Crypto investors face a liquidity dilemma. Their wealth sits in volatile assets they genuinely believe in for the long term, but when they actually need cash, they find themselves stuck with some pretty bad options. They can sell at potentially the worst possible time, or they can go hat in hand to banks begging for permission to borrow, or they can risk getting liquidated through crypto lending platforms. The frustrating thing is that none of these methods actually lets you securely keep your position while getting the liquidity you need.

THE SOLUTION:

A properly designed whole life insurance policy creates a parallel capital base that exists completely separately from your crypto holdings. The cash value grows steadily regardless of what crypto markets are doing, and when you need liquidity, policy loans give you tax-free access to that capital without selling anything or asking anyone for permission. Meanwhile, your crypto stays exactly where it belongs in secure custody, which means you capture all the future upside you believe is coming.

THE MECHANICS:

The mechanics work like this: your premiums fund the policy over time, and then guaranteed interest along with dividends grow the cash value while paid-up additions accelerate that growth even further. When you need money, policy loans give you access to capital that's secured by your cash value, and the flexible repayment terms let you match your loan management to your actual cash flow rather than some arbitrary schedule imposed by a lender. What makes the whole system so powerful is that this cycle can repeat throughout your entire life.

THE REQUIREMENTS:

- Stable income to sustain premiums for years
- Patience to wait for cash value to build
- Discipline to manage loans responsibly
- Capital beyond immediate needs
- Willingness to learn something unfamiliar

THE DESIGN PRINCIPLES:

- Maximize cash value, not death benefit
- Use paid-up additions to accelerate growth
- Stay below MEC limits to preserve tax advantages
- Choose carriers with financial strength and dividend track records

- Understand loan provisions before you need them
- Work with advisors who understand the strategy

THE COORDINATION:

- Fund premiums consistently regardless of crypto market conditions
- Use policy loans to avoid taxable sales of crypto
- Repay loans during periods of strength
- Monitor loan-to-cash-value ratios to prevent lapse risk
- Integrate the policy with broader financial and estate planning

THE LONG VIEW:

The first few years feel slow, maybe even frustrating. You're putting money in and not seeing much to show for it. But that's how compounding works. It crawls, then it walks, then it runs. The people who stick with it end up with a financial tool that grows with them through every stage of life. What starts as a liquidity backup in your 30s becomes a cornerstone of your wealth architecture by your 50s. The key is staying engaged, keeping an eye on it, and not letting it drift into neglect. Managed well, this thing works for you for the rest of your life. Ignored, it can become a problem. The difference is attention.

THE HONEST ASSESSMENT:

Let's be honest about what this requires. You need capital to fund premiums. You need patience to wait years before borrowing capacity becomes meaningful. You need to pay attention and actually manage the thing. You're trusting an insurance company, which means counterparty risk exists.

The returns on cash value won't compete with a bull market in crypto. And yes, it's more complicated than just holding coins and hoping for the best. But you're also getting something in return.

If you're sitting on significant crypto holdings, if you believe in where this is going long-term, and if you know that life will eventually demand liquidity at an inconvenient time, this solves a problem that doesn't have many good solutions. You get to stay in your positions when everyone else is forced to sell. You get options precisely when options are hardest to come by.

Your crypto stays in secure custody, exposure stays intact and the upside stays yours. The policy is the infrastructure that makes all of that possible.

INFINITE BANKING FOR CRYPTO INVESTORS

SO NOW WHAT?

Throughout this book, you've learned the concepts, the mechanics, the design principles, the timing strategies, and the philosophical framework that makes all of this work. You've seen the pitfalls and the red flags. You've got the vocabulary and the quick references you'll need going forward.

Now you understand something that most crypto investors never even consider. You see the liquidity trap for what it really is, and you know there's a fourth option beyond selling, bank loans, and crypto lending. You have the knowledge to evaluate policies, question advisors, and build a system that actually serves your goals.

That knowledge changes how you experience volatility in a pretty profound way. You stop fearing liquidity needs because you know you have options. You stop calculating which positions you'd have to sacrifice if something comes up. You stop experiencing every price drop as a potential crisis that might force your hand.

What this gives you is the ability to operate from a position of strength. Your financial decisions start reflecting your actual investment thesis rather than some desperate scramble for cash. Your conviction can finally manifest in action because you have the infrastructure to support it through whatever the market throws at you.

The system you build has two engines running in parallel, each serving a different purpose. Your crypto holdings capture growth, sitting in self-custody, positioned for whatever upside the market delivers. Your policy cash value provides stability, growing predictably, accessible through loans whenever you need liquidity. You don't have to choose between conviction and cash flow anymore. You can have both working together.

That's what financial sovereignty really means when you think about it. It goes beyond just having custody of your keys to include genuine control over your decisions and your timing. It means having ownership of assets along with the ability to maintain that ownership through whatever circumstances arise.

The crypto community talks about being your own bank. This strategy takes that idea seriously and gives you the tools to actually make it happen.

WHAT HAPPENS NEXT IS UP TO YOU

The hardest part of this strategy isn't understanding the math. It's finding a partner who actually understands the intersection of whole life insurance and cryptocurrency. Most insurance agents will gloss over crypto compliance. Most crypto natives don't understand actuarial design. The professionals who excel at both are rare.

THIS IS WHY DIGITAL ASCENSION GROUP EXISTS

We work with billions of dollars in digital assets. We've built the network of professionals who understand both worlds. We know which carriers work with crypto investors, which policy designs optimize for your situation, and how to integrate this framework into your existing wealth architecture.

You don't have to build this alone. You shouldn't rely on generalists for a specialist's job. Run the numbers. Test the scenarios. Verify the assumptions. Then decide.

Infinite Banking requires capital, time, discipline, and a willingness to learn something that sits outside normal crypto discourse. It's not for everyone. But for the right person with the right circumstances, it changes how you think about wealth entirely.

You already chose sovereignty when you chose crypto. Now extend that sovereignty to your liquidity.

Visit www.DAGFamilyOffice.com to start the conversation.

Let's build it.

INFINITE BANKING FOR CRYPTO INVESTORS

APPENDIX A: GLOSSARY OF KEY TERMS

CASH VALUE:

The accumulated savings component inside a whole life insurance policy. Grows through premium payments, guaranteed interest, and dividend crediting. Can be borrowed against through policy loans.

DEATH BENEFIT:

The amount paid to beneficiaries when the insured person dies. Reduced by any outstanding policy loans.

DIRECT RECOGNITION:

A method where the insurance company reduces dividend crediting on cash value that's been borrowed against. Less favorable for active borrowers.

DIVIDEND:

Annual distribution from insurance company surplus to participating policy holders. Not guaranteed but historically consistent from major mutual insurers.

INFINITE BANKING FOR CRYPTO INVESTORS

GUARANTEED INTEREST RATE:

The minimum rate the insurance company must credit to your cash value per the contract. Typically 3-4%.

MODIFIED ENDOWMENT CONTRACT (MEC):

A life insurance policy that has received too much premium relative to death benefit, losing favorable tax treatment of loans and withdrawals.

MUTUAL INSURANCE COMPANY:

An insurance company owned by its policyholders rather than shareholders. Surplus is distributed to policyholders as dividends.

NON-DIRECT RECOGNITION:

A method where dividend crediting continues at full rates regardless of outstanding loans. More favorable for active borrowers.

PAID-UP ADDITIONS (PUA):

Additional whole life insurance purchased with extra premiums or dividends. Immediately increases cash value and death benefit.

PARTICIPATING POLICY:

A whole life policy that participates in company surplus through dividend payments. Required for Infinite Banking.

POLICY LOAN:

A loan from the insurance company secured by your policy's cash value. Not a withdrawal, so cash value continues earning. Generally tax-free.

PREMIUM:

The payment you make to fund your insurance policy. Base premium keeps the policy in force. PUA premium accelerates cash value growth.

SURRENDER VALUE:

The amount you would receive if you canceled the policy. Cash value minus any surrender charges.

7-PAY TEST:

An IRS test determining if a policy is a MEC. Compares cumulative premiums to a limit based on death benefit over seven years.

INFINITE BANKING FOR CRYPTO INVESTORS

APPENDIX B: DECISION CHECKLIST

BEFORE IMPLEMENTING THE STRATEGY:

- Stable income to sustain premiums for 5+ years minimum
- Existing crypto holdings committed to long-term holding
- Capital beyond immediate needs and emergency reserves
- Patience for 3-5 year timeline before meaningful borrowing capacity
- Willingness to learn unfamiliar concepts
- No need for liquidity in the next 12-24 months

WHEN SELECTING AN ADVISOR:

- Specializes in Infinite Banking, not just general insurance
- Can explain compensation structure clearly
- Willing to show multiple carrier illustrations
- Understands MEC implications and can explain clearly
- Experience with crypto investors preferred
- No pressure tactics or rushing

INFINITE BANKING FOR CRYPTO INVESTORS

WHEN EVALUATING A POLICY:

- Cash value focused design, not death benefit maximized
- High PUA capacity relative to base premium
- Competitive loan interest rate
- Non-direct recognition preferred
- Guaranteed values provide reasonable floor
- Illustrated assumptions match recent actual dividend rates

WHEN SELECTING A CARRIER:

- Financial strength ratings A or better
- 20+ year dividend payment history
- Dividend consistency through stress periods (2008-2009)
- Favorable loan provisions
- Good reputation for policyholder service
- Reasonable loan processing speed

ONGOING MANAGEMENT:

- Annual review of in-force illustration
- Loan-to-cash-value ratio monitored (keep below 70-80%)
- At minimum, annual interest paid on loans
- Premium payments maintained consistently
- PUA contributions adjusted based on circumstances
- Repayment triggers defined and followed

APPENDIX B: DECISION CHECKLIST

INFINITE BANKING FOR CRYPTO INVESTORS

APPENDIX C: FURTHER RESOURCES

RATING AGENCIES:

A.M. Best (ambest.com) - Insurance company ratings and analysis

Moody's (moodys.com) - Financial strength ratings

S&P Global (spglobal.com) - Insurance company ratings

FOUNDATIONAL READING

Becoming Your Own Banker by Nelson Nash - the original Infinite Banking text, should be required reading

The Case for IBC by R. Nelson Nash - shorter, more accessible entry point

Bank On Yourself by Pamela Yellen - controversial in IBC circles but offers a different perspective worth understanding

What Would the Rockefellers Do? by Garrett Gunderson - covers how wealthy families have used this strategy for generations

POLICY ANALYSIS TOOLS

Truth Concepts software - the calculator most serious IBC practitioners use to model scenarios

Infinite Banking Calculator (infinitebanking.org has one) - basic modeling tool

IRR calculators - to compare true internal rate of return across policy options

INFINITE BANKING FOR CRYPTO INVESTORS

ENDNOTES & BIBLIOGRAPHY

ENDNOTES - INTRODUCTION

Chainalysis, The 2020 State of Crypto Crime Report (New York: Chainalysis Inc., 2020). See also Jeff John Roberts, "Nearly 4 Million Bitcoins Lost Forever, New Study Says," Fortune, November 25, 2017.

R. Nelson Nash, Becoming Your Own Banker: Unlock the Infinite Banking Concept, 1st ed. (Birmingham, AL: Infinite Banking Concepts, LLC, 2000).

ENDNOTES - CHAPTER 1: THE LIQUIDITY PROBLEM

Dirk G. Baur and Thomas Dimpfl, "The Volatility of Bitcoin and Its Role as a Medium of Exchange and a Store of Value," Empirical Economics 61 (2021): 2663–2683.

Yukun Liu and Aleh Tsyvinski, "Risks and Returns of Cryptocurrency," The Review of Financial Studies 34, no. 6 (2021): 2689–2727.

David Yermack, "Is Bitcoin a Real Currency? An Economic Appraisal," in Handbook of Digital Currency, ed. David Lee Kuo Chuen (San Diego: Academic Press, 2015), 31–43.

Consumer Financial Protection Bureau, Building Emergency Savings (Washington, DC: CFPB, 2023), https://www.consumerfinance.gov.

Alicia H. Munnell, Anthony Webb, and Francesca Golub-Sass, "The National Retirement Risk Index: An Update," Center for Retirement Research at Boston College, Issue Brief 12-20 (October 2012).

Board of Governors of the Federal Reserve System, Senior Loan Officer Opinion Survey on Bank Lending Practices (Washington, DC: Federal Reserve, 2024).

Victoria Ivashina and David Scharfstein, "Bank Lending During the Financial Crisis of 2008," Journal of Financial Economics 97, no. 3 (September 2010): 319–338.

Ben S. Bernanke and Cara S. Lown, "The Credit Crunch," Brookings Papers on Economic Activity 1991, no. 2 (1991): 205–247.

Lewis Gudgeon, Daniel Perez, Dominik Harz, Benjamin Livshits, and Arthur Gervais, "The Decentralized Financial Crisis," 2020 Crypto Valley Conference on Blockchain Technology (2020): 1–15.

Kaihua Qin, Liyi Zhou, Benjamin Livshits, and Arthur Gervais, "Attacking the DeFi Ecosystem with Flash Loans for Fun and Profit," Financial Cryptography and Data Security 2021 (Berlin: Springer, 2021).

Daniel Perez, Sam M. Werner, Jiahua Xu, and Benjamin Livshits, "Liquidations: DeFi on a Knife-edge," Financial Cryptography and Data Security 2021 (Berlin: Springer, 2021).

Chainalysis, The 2023 Crypto Crime Report (New York: Chainalysis Inc., 2023).

Nicola Atzei, Massimo Bartoletti, and Tiziana Cimoli, "A Survey of Attacks on Ethereum Smart Contracts," Principles of Security and Trust (Berlin: Springer, 2017), 164–186.

ENDNOTES - CHAPTER 2: HOW INFINITE BANKING WORKS

Northwestern Mutual, 2024 Annual Report (Milwaukee: Northwestern Mutual, 2024). Northwestern Mutual has paid dividends consecutively since 1872.

MassMutual, Policyholder Dividend History (Springfield, MA: MassMutual, 2024). MassMutual has paid dividends since 1869.

New York Life, Company History and Dividend Record (New York: New York Life Insurance Company, 2024). New York Life has paid dividends since 1854.

American Council of Life Insurers, Life Insurers Fact Book (Washington, DC: ACLI, 2023).

Society of Actuaries, "Guaranteed Interest Rates in Whole Life Insurance Products," SOA Research Reports (Schaumburg, IL: Society of Actuaries, 2022).

Internal Revenue Code § 72(e)(5), "Treatment of amounts received on policy loans."

Internal Revenue Service, Publication 525: Taxable and Nontaxable Income (Washington, DC: Department of the Treasury, 2024).

Howard Zaritsky, Tax Planning for Family Wealth Transfers, 5th ed. (Eagan, MN: Thomson Reuters, 2023).

Internal Revenue Code § 7702A, "Modified Endowment Contracts Defined."

Technical and Miscellaneous Revenue Act of 1988 (TAMRA), Pub. L. No. 100-647.

Internal Revenue Service, Notice 88-128, "Guidance on Modified Endowment Contracts" (1988).

Internal Revenue Code § 72(e)(4)(A), "Treatment of policy loans in excess of basis."

Minnis v. Commissioner, T.C. Memo. 2015-9 (2015).

National Association of Insurance Commissioners, U.S. Life Insurance Industry Investment Portfolio Summary (Kansas City, MO: NAIC Capital Markets Bureau, 2023).

American Council of Life Insurers, Life Insurers Fact Book, Chapter 6: Assets (Washington, DC: ACLI, 2023).

Society of Actuaries, "Historical Analysis of Participating Whole Life Dividend Scales," SOA Research Reports (Schaumburg, IL: Society of Actuaries, 2019).

J. David Cummins and Bertrand Venard, eds., Handbook of International Insurance (New York: Springer, 2007).

National Association of Insurance Commissioners, Variable Life Insurance Model Regulation (Model #270) (Kansas City, MO: NAIC, 2022).

ENDNOTES - CHAPTER 3: DESIGNING A POLICY THAT ACTUALLY WORKS

David Mayers and Clifford W. Smith Jr., "Ownership Structure Across Lines of Property-Casualty Insurance," Journal of Law and Economics 31, no. 2 (October 1988): 351–378.

Henry Hansmann, "The Organization of Insurance Companies: Mutual versus Stock," Journal of Law, Economics, & Organization 1, no. 1 (Spring 1985): 125–153.

A.M. Best Company, Best's Credit Rating Methodology (Oldwick, NJ: A.M. Best Rating Services, 2024).

Moody's Investors Service, Rating Methodology: Life Insurers (New York: Moody's, 2024).

S&P Global Ratings, Insurer Financial Strength Ratings Definitions (New York: S&P Global, 2024).

Michael R. Blease and David A. Duff, "Policy Loan Recognition Methods and Their Impact on Whole Life Performance," Journal of Financial Service Professionals 73, no. 4 (2019): 68–77.

Stephan R. Leimberg et al., Tools & Techniques of Life Insurance Planning, 8th ed. (Erlanger, KY: National Underwriter Company, 2023).

James M. Carson and Mark D. Forster, "Agent Compensation and Sales Practices in the Life Insurance Industry," Journal of Insurance Regulation 19, no. 2 (2000): 223–247.

Nadine Gatzert and Hato Schmeiser, "The Merits of Pooling Claims: Mutual versus Stock Insurers," Journal of Risk and Insurance 79, no. 2 (2012): 529–554.

ENDNOTES - CHAPTER 4: COORDINATING WITH YOUR CRYPTO HOLDINGS

National Institute of Standards and Technology, FIPS 140-2: Security Requirements for Cryptographic Modules (Washington, DC: U.S. Department of Commerce, 2019).

National Institute of Standards and Technology, FIPS 140-3: Security Requirements for Cryptographic Modules (Washington, DC: U.S. Department of Commerce, 2019).

Office of the Comptroller of the Currency, Interpretive Letter #1170, "Authority of a National Bank to Provide Cryptocurrency Custody Services" (July 22, 2020).

Office of the Comptroller of the Currency, "Anchorage Digital Bank National Association Charter Approval," OCC News Release 2021-6 (January 13, 2021).

Nevada Financial Institutions Division, Order Taking Possession of Prime Trust, LLC (Carson City, NV: State of Nevada, 2023).

U.S. Securities and Exchange Commission, "SEC Charges Samuel Bankman-Fried with Defrauding Investors in Crypto Asset Trading Platform FTX," SEC Press Release 2022-219 (December 13, 2022).

United States Bankruptcy Court, Southern District of New York, In re: FTX Trading Ltd., Case No. 22-11068 (2022).

United States Bankruptcy Court, Southern District of New York, In re: Celsius Network LLC, Case No. 22-10964 (2022).

United States Bankruptcy Court, Southern District of New Jersey, In re: Voyager Digital Holdings, Inc., Case No. 22-10943 (2022).

National Organization of Life & Health Insurance Guaranty Associations, State Life and Health Insurance Guaranty Association Coverage Limits (Herndon, VA: NOLHGA, 2024), https://www.nolhga.com.

National Association of Insurance Commissioners, Life and Health Insurance Guaranty Association Model Act (Model #520) (Kansas City, MO: NAIC, 2023).

Internal Revenue Service, Notice 2014-21, "IRS Virtual Currency Guidance" (Washington, DC: Department of the Treasury, 2014).

Internal Revenue Service, Publication 544: Sales and Other Dispositions of Assets (Washington, DC: Department of the Treasury, 2023).

Internal Revenue Service, "Topic No. 409: Capital Gains and Losses" (2024), https://www.irs.gov.

Internal Revenue Service, Frequently Asked Questions on Virtual Currency Transactions (2024), https://www.irs.gov.

Internal Revenue Service, Revenue Ruling 2019-24, "Tax Treatment of Cryptocurrency Hard Forks" (2019).

Infrastructure Investment and Jobs Act of 2021, Pub. L. No. 117-58.

ENDNOTES - CHAPTER 5: THINKING IN DECADES

Joseph M. Belth, Life Insurance: A Consumer's Handbook, 2nd ed. (Bloomington: Indiana University Press, 1985).

Ben G. Baldwin, The New Life Insurance Investment Advisor, 2nd ed. (New York: McGraw-Hill, 2002).

Jason S. Scott, John G. Watson, and Wei Hu, "Efficient Annuitization: Optimal Strategies for Hedging Mortality Risk," Pension Research Council Working Paper (2007).

Richard H. Thaler and Shlomo Benartzi, "Save More Tomorrow: Using Behavioral Economics to Increase Employee Saving," Journal of Political Economy 112, no. S1 (February 2004): S164–S187.

James J. Choi, David Laibson, Brigitte C. Madrian, and Andrew Metrick, "For Better or for Worse: Default Effects and 401(k) Savings Behavior," in Perspectives on the Economics of Aging, ed. David A. Wise (Chicago: University of Chicago Press, 2004), 81–126.

Annamaria Lusardi and Olivia S. Mitchell, "The Economic Importance of Financial Literacy: Theory and Evidence," Journal of Economic Literature 52, no. 1 (March 2014): 5–44.

National Organization of Life & Health Insurance Guaranty Associations, History of Life Insurance Company Insolvencies (Herndon, VA: NOLHGA, 2023).

J. David Cummins, "Risk-Based Premiums for Insurance Guaranty Funds," Journal of Finance 43, no. 4 (September 1988): 823–839.

Robert W. Klein, "Insurance Regulation in Transition," Journal of Risk and Insurance 62, no. 3 (September 1995): 363–404.

Elijah Brewer III and Thomas S. Mondschean, "An Empirical Test of the Incentive Effects of Deposit Insurance," Journal of Money, Credit and Banking 26, no. 1 (February 1994): 146–164.

Scott E. Harrington, "The Financial Crisis, Systemic Risk, and the Future of Insurance Regulation," Journal of Risk and Insurance 76, no. 4 (December 2009): 785–819.

Geneva Association, Systemic Risk in Insurance: An Analysis of Insurance and Financial Stability, The Geneva Reports (Geneva: The Geneva Association, 2010).

Endnotes - Chapter 6: Estate Planning Considerations

Internal Revenue Code § 101(a)(1), "Gross income does not include amounts received... under a life insurance contract, if such amounts are paid by reason of the death of the insured."

Internal Revenue Code § 2042, "Proceeds of Life Insurance."

Crummey v. Commissioner, 397 F.2d 82 (9th Cir. 1968).

Howard Zaritsky and Stephan R. Leimberg, Tax Planning with Life Insurance, 3rd ed. (Eagan, MN: Thomson Reuters, 2023).

Internal Revenue Code § 2056, "Bequests to Surviving Spouse (Unlimited Marital Deduction)."

Internal Revenue Code § 1035, "Certain Exchanges of Insurance Policies."

Internal Revenue Service, Revenue Ruling 2008-40, "Partial 1035 Exchanges" (2008).

Internal Revenue Code § 401(a)(9), "Required Distributions."

Internal Revenue Service, Publication 590-B: Distributions from Individual Retirement Arrangements (IRAs) (Washington, DC: Department of the Treasury, 2024).

Setting Every Community Up for Retirement Enhancement Act of 2019 (SECURE Act), Pub. L. No. 116-94, Division O.

SECURE 2.0 Act of 2022, Pub. L. No. 117-328, Division T.

ENDNOTES - REGULATORY FRAMEWORK

McCarran-Ferguson Act of 1945, 15 U.S.C. §§ 1011–1015.

National Association of Insurance Commissioners, Insurance Regulation 101 (Kansas City, MO: NAIC, 2023).

Robert W. Klein, "Principles for Insurance Regulation: An Evaluation of Current Practices and Potential Reforms," Geneva Papers on Risk and Insurance 37, no. 1 (January 2012): 175–199.

U.S. Securities and Exchange Commission, Framework for "Investment Contract" Analysis of Digital Assets (Washington, DC: SEC, 2019).

Financial Crimes Enforcement Network, Application of FinCEN's Regulations to Certain Business Models Involving Convertible Virtual Currencies, Guidance FIN-2019-G001 (May 9, 2019).

Commodity Futures Trading Commission, Digital Assets Primer (Washington, DC: CFTC, 2023).

BIBLIOGRAPHY - TAX LAW AND IRS GUIDANCE

Internal Revenue Code §§ 72, 101, 401, 1035, 1091, 2042, 2056, 7702A.

Internal Revenue Service. Notice 2014-21: IRS Virtual Currency Guidance. Washington, DC: Department of the Treasury, 2014.

Internal Revenue Service. Notice 88-128: Guidance on Modified Endowment Contracts. 1988.

Internal Revenue Service. Publication 525: Taxable and Nontaxable Income. Washington, DC: Department of the Treasury, 2024.

Internal Revenue Service. Publication 544: Sales and Other Dispositions of Assets. Washington, DC: Department of the Treasury, 2023.

Internal Revenue Service. Publication 590-B: Distributions from Individual Retirement Arrangements (IRAs). Washington, DC: Department of the Treasury, 2024.

Internal Revenue Service. Revenue Ruling 2008-40: Partial 1035 Exchanges. 2008.

Internal Revenue Service. Revenue Ruling 2019-24: Tax Treatment of Cryptocurrency Hard Forks. 2019.

BIBLIOGRAPHY - INSURANCE REGULATION AND INDUSTRY STANDARDS

A.M. Best Company. Best's Credit Rating Methodology. Oldwick, NJ: A.M. Best Rating Services, 2024.

American Council of Life Insurers. Life Insurers Fact Book. Washington, DC: ACLI, 2023.

Moody's Investors Service. Rating Methodology: Life Insurers. New York: Moody's, 2024.

National Association of Insurance Commissioners. Insurance Regulation 101. Kansas City, MO: NAIC, 2023.

National Association of Insurance Commissioners. Life and Health Insurance Guaranty Association Model Act (Model #520). Kansas City, MO: NAIC, 2023.

National Association of Insurance Commissioners. U.S. Life Insurance Industry Investment Portfolio Summary. Kansas City, MO: NAIC Capital Markets Bureau, 2023.

National Association of Insurance Commissioners. Variable Life Insurance Model Regulation (Model #270). Kansas City, MO: NAIC, 2022.

National Organization of Life & Health Insurance Guaranty Associations. History of Life Insurance Company Insolvencies. Herndon, VA: NOLHGA, 2023.

National Organization of Life & Health Insurance Guaranty Associations. State Life and Health Insurance Guaranty Association Coverage Limits. Herndon, VA: NOLHGA, 2024.

S&P Global Ratings. Insurer Financial Strength Ratings Definitions. New York: S&P Global, 2024.

Society of Actuaries. "Guaranteed Interest Rates in Whole Life Insurance Products." SOA Research Reports. Schaumburg, IL: Society of Actuaries, 2022.

Society of Actuaries. "Historical Analysis of Participating Whole Life Dividend Scales." SOA Research Reports. Schaumburg, IL: Society of Actuaries, 2019.

Cryptocurrency Regulatory Materials

Commodity Futures Trading Commission. Digital Assets Primer. Washington, DC: CFTC, 2023.

Financial Crimes Enforcement Network. Application of FinCEN's Regulations to Certain Business Models Involving Convertible Virtual Currencies. Guidance FIN-2019-G001. May 9, 2019.

National Institute of Standards and Technology. FIPS 140-2: Security Requirements for Cryptographic Modules. Washington, DC: U.S. Department of Commerce, 2019.

National Institute of Standards and Technology. FIPS 140-3: Security Requirements for Cryptographic Modules. Washington, DC: U.S. Department of Commerce, 2019.

Office of the Comptroller of the Currency. Interpretive Letter #1170: Authority of a National Bank to Provide Cryptocurrency Custody Services. July 22, 2020.

U.S. Securities and Exchange Commission. Framework for "Investment Contract" Analysis of Digital Assets. Washington, DC: SEC, 2019.

BIBLIOGRAPHY - ACADEMIC AND PROFESSIONAL TEXTS

Antonopoulos, Andreas M. Mastering Bitcoin: Programming the Open Blockchain. 2nd ed. Sebastopol, CA: O'Reilly Media, 2017.

Baldwin, Ben G. The New Life Insurance Investment Advisor. 2nd ed. New York: McGraw-Hill, 2002.

Belth, Joseph M. Life Insurance: A Consumer's Handbook. 2nd ed. Bloomington: Indiana University Press, 1985.

Black, Kenneth, and Harold D. Skipper Jr. Life Insurance. 14th ed. Lucretian, LLC, 2015.

Cummins, J. David, and Bertrand Venard, eds. Handbook of International Insurance. New York: Springer, 2007.

Leimberg, Stephan R., et al. Tools & Techniques of Life Insurance Planning. 8th ed. Erlanger, KY: National Underwriter Company, 2023.

Narayanan, Arvind, Joseph Bonneau, Edward Felten, Andrew Miller, and Steven Goldfeder. Bitcoin and Cryptocurrency Technologies. Princeton, NJ: Princeton University Press, 2016.

Nash, R. Nelson. Becoming Your Own Banker: Unlock the Infinite Banking Concept. 1st ed. Birmingham, AL: Infinite Banking Concepts, LLC, 2000.

Song, Jimmy. Programming Bitcoin: Learn How to Program Bitcoin from Scratch. Sebastopol, CA: O'Reilly Media, 2019.

Zaritsky, Howard. Tax Planning for Family Wealth Transfers. 5th ed. Eagan, MN: Thomson Reuters, 2023.

Zaritsky, Howard, and Stephan R. Leimberg. Tax Planning with Life Insurance. 3rd ed. Eagan, MN: Thomson Reuters, 2023.

BIBLIOGRAPHY - COURT CASES

Crummey v. Commissioner, 397 F.2d 82 (9th Cir. 1968).

Minnis v. Commissioner, T.C. Memo. 2015-9 (2015).

BIBLIOGRAPHY - FEDERAL LEGISLATION

Infrastructure Investment and Jobs Act of 2021, Pub. L. No. 117-58.

McCarran-Ferguson Act of 1945, 15 U.S.C. §§ 1011–1015.

SECURE 2.0 Act of 2022, Pub. L. No. 117-328, Division T.

Setting Every Community Up for Retirement Enhancement Act of 2019 (SECURE Act), Pub. L. No. 116-94, Division O.

Technical and Miscellaneous Revenue Act of 1988 (TAMRA), Pub. L. No. 100-647.

BIBLIOGRAPHY - BANKRUPTCY PROCEEDINGS

United States Bankruptcy Court, Southern District of New Jersey. In re: Voyager Digital Holdings, Inc. Case No. 22-10943. 2022.

United States Bankruptcy Court, Southern District of New York. In re: Celsius Network LLC. Case No. 22-10964. 2022.

United States Bankruptcy Court, Southern District of New York. In re: FTX Trading Ltd. Case No. 22-11068. 2022.

BIBLIOGRAPHY - INDUSTRY REPORTS AND RESEARCH

Baur, Dirk G., and Thomas Dimpfl. "The Volatility of Bitcoin and Its Role as a Medium of Exchange and a Store of Value." Empirical Economics 61 (2021): 2663–2683.

Bernanke, Ben S., and Cara S. Lown. "The Credit Crunch." Brookings Papers on Economic Activity 1991, no. 2 (1991): 205–247.

Blease, Michael R., and David A. Duff. "Policy Loan Recognition Methods and Their Impact on Whole Life Performance." Journal of Financial Service Professionals 73, no. 4 (2019): 68–77.

Brewer, Elijah III, and Thomas S. Mondschean. "An Empirical Test of the Incentive Effects of Deposit Insurance." Journal of Money, Credit and Banking 26, no. 1 (February 1994): 146–164.

Carson, James M., and Mark D. Forster. "Agent Compensation and Sales Practices in the Life Insurance Industry." Journal of Insurance Regulation 19, no. 2 (2000): 223–247.

Chainalysis. The 2020 State of Crypto Crime Report. New York: Chainalysis Inc., 2020.

Chainalysis. The 2023 Crypto Crime Report. New York: Chainalysis Inc., 2023.

Choi, James J., David Laibson, Brigitte C. Madrian, and Andrew Metrick. "For Better or for Worse: Default Effects and 401(k) Savings Behavior." In Perspectives on the Economics of Aging, edited by David A. Wise, 81–126. Chicago: University of Chicago Press, 2004.

Cummins, J. David. "Risk-Based Premiums for Insurance Guaranty Funds." Journal of Finance 43, no. 4 (September 1988): 823–839.

Gatzert, Nadine, and Hato Schmeiser. "The Merits of Pooling Claims: Mutual versus Stock Insurers." Journal of Risk and Insurance 79, no. 2 (2012): 529–554.

Geneva Association. Systemic Risk in Insurance: An Analysis of Insurance and Financial Stability. The Geneva Reports. Geneva: The Geneva Association, 2010.

Gudgeon, Lewis, Daniel Perez, Dominik Harz, Benjamin Livshits, and Arthur Gervais. "The Decentralized Financial Crisis." 2020 Crypto Valley Conference on Blockchain Technology (2020): 1–15.

Hansmann, Henry. "The Organization of Insurance Companies: Mutual versus Stock." Journal of Law, Economics, & Organization 1, no. 1 (Spring 1985): 125–153.

Harrington, Scott E. "The Financial Crisis, Systemic Risk, and the Future of Insurance Regulation." Journal of Risk and Insurance 76, no. 4 (December 2009): 785–819.

Ivashina, Victoria, and David Scharfstein. "Bank Lending During the Financial Crisis of 2008." Journal of Financial Economics 97, no. 3 (September 2010): 319–338.

Klein, Robert W. "Insurance Regulation in Transition." Journal of Risk and Insurance 62, no. 3 (September 1995): 363–404.

Klein, Robert W. "Principles for Insurance Regulation: An Evaluation of Current Practices and Potential Reforms." Geneva Papers on Risk and Insurance 37, no. 1 (January 2012): 175–199.

Liu, Yukun, and Aleh Tsyvinski. "Risks and Returns of Cryptocurrency." The Review of Financial Studies 34, no. 6 (2021): 2689–2727.

Lusardi, Annamaria, and Olivia S. Mitchell. "The Economic Importance of Financial Literacy: Theory and Evidence." Journal of Economic Literature 52, no. 1 (March 2014): 5–44.

Mayers, David, and Clifford W. Smith Jr. "Ownership Structure Across Lines of Property-Casualty Insurance." Journal of Law and Economics 31, no. 2 (October 1988): 351–378.

Munnell, Alicia H., Anthony Webb, and Francesca Golub-Sass. "The National Retirement Risk Index: An Update." Center for Retirement Research at Boston College, Issue Brief 12-20. October 2012.

Perez, Daniel, Sam M. Werner, Jiahua Xu, and Benjamin Livshits. "Liquidations: DeFi on a Knife-edge." Financial Cryptography and Data Security 2021. Berlin: Springer, 2021.

Qin, Kaihua, Liyi Zhou, Benjamin Livshits, and Arthur Gervais. "Attacking the DeFi Ecosystem with Flash Loans for Fun and Profit." Financial Cryptography and Data Security 2021. Berlin: Springer, 2021.

Scott, Jason S., John G. Watson, and Wei Hu. "Efficient Annuitization: Optimal Strategies for Hedging Mortality Risk." Pension Research Council Working Paper. 2007.

Thaler, Richard H., and Shlomo Benartzi. "Save More Tomorrow: Using Behavioral Economics to Increase Employee Saving." Journal of Political Economy 112, no. S1 (February 2004): S164–S187.

Yermack, David. "Is Bitcoin a Real Currency? An Economic Appraisal." In Handbook of Digital Currency, edited by David Lee Kuo Chuen, 31–43. San Diego: Academic Press, 2015.

Note: All URLs were accessible at the time of publication. Regulatory guidance and industry data are subject to periodic updates. Readers should verify current provisions with authoritative sources.

Made in United States
Orlando, FL
26 December 2025